FAMILY JOKE BOOK

MIKE YARWOOD

AF574757

Hamlyn Paperbacks

FAMILY JOKE BOOK

ISBN 0 600 20104 X

First published in Great Britain 1980
by Hamlyn Paperbacks
Copyright © 1980 by Victorama Ltd

Hamlyn Paperbacks are published by
The Hamlyn Publishing Group Ltd,
Astronaut House,
Feltham,
Middlesex, England
(Paperback Division: Hamlyn Paperbacks,
Banda House, Cambridge Grove,
Hammersmith, London W6 OLE)

Made and printed in Great Britain by
Hunt Barnard Printing Ltd, Aylesbury, Bucks

This book is sold subject to the condition that it shall not, by way of trade or otherwise, be lent, re-sold, hired out, or otherwise circulated without the publisher's prior consent in any form of binding or cover other than that in which it is published and without a similar condition including this condition being imposed on the subsequent purchaser.

MIKE YARWOOD

Mike Yarwood was only five when he began displaying his talent for mimicry. He became a full-time entertainer at the age of twenty - since when he has established himself as one of the brightest stars in showbusiness, with three Royal Variety Shows, a season at the London Palladium and numerous highly successful TV series to his credit. Through his TV shows he has become a household name, and his impersonations of Sir Harold Wilson, Margaret Thatcher and Prince Charles have become classics. In 1976 he was awarded the O.B.E.

Mike Yarwood lives in Prestbury, Cheshire, with his wife Sandra and their two daughters Charlotte and Clare.

CONTENTS

INTRODUCTION

Welcome to my *Family Joke Book.*

I'm Mike Yarwood – yes, really – and here you will find jokes galore dedicated to all the members of my family, from my nearest and dearest to the long-lost relatives who have been lost so long that even Eamonn Andrews and the *This is Your Life* team couldn't find them!

Rather like my family, the jokes in the book come in all shapes and sizes. There are long ones and short ones, old ones and new ones, funny ones and very funny ones. They make me and my family laugh: I hope they will make you and yours laugh too.

What else makes me laugh?

Well, I enjoy all kinds of humour, whether it is American situation comedy, which is so very witty and never blue, or Morecambe and Wise, who are the undoubted masters of timing. Jack Lemmon is someone I greatly admire. I appreciate him as a straight actor but he is at his most brilliant in comedy, especially when he is working with a Neil Simon script like *The Odd Couple. Monty Python* makes me laugh particularly when the team is being very silly; I love good slapstick. Peter Sellers is another favourite of mine: he manages to be hilariously funny without ever going over the top.

As a child, I used to love visual comedy. I think all kids do because often they don't understand verbal humour. We used to go to the pantomime at the Stockport Theatre and I can remember one time when I was very young, being taken to see the Chaplin film, *Limelight*. Charlie seemed to be growing enormously long legs, and I actually cried with laughing. Max Wall did a similar kind of visual gag on an early television programme, with one arm getting longer. That was the funniest mute comedy I have ever seen.

When it comes to life you can't plan something funny, it just depends on the right moment. It's spontaneity that counts – that's why children can be so funny. I find myself using other people's voices in off-the-cuff situations like that. My wife Sandra and I were watching a television programme about nudists one day. Some woman was saying 'Has anyone here seen Willie?'. I just remarked in my best Prince Charles voice: 'Rather an unfortunate name for a nudist, wouldn't you say?' Sandra fell about laughing, but I don't suppose it would have been half as funny if I had used my own voice. I retreat behind my characters, too, sometimes. For example, if I have to give somebody a ticking off I use my Harold Wilson voice.

Not every family has to deal with all the interlopers my family suffers from. I suppose Sandra has learnt to live with half the House of Commons, as I do tend to take people home with me when I am learning a new character. I remember just after I had started learning Prince Charles, Sandra and I were invited to a private dinner party where he was a guest. Sandra was sitting next to him at table. He asked if I practised at home and she replied 'Yes, I've been living with you for the last three weeks.' He very courteously replied, 'I wish I'd known.'

I never intend to be disrespectful about the people I impersonate, though I sometimes wonder whether they take it in such good part themselves. Sir Harold Wilson is the only one who was really open about being a member of my 'clientele', as he called it. Patrick Moore gave me 'ten out of ten' for the voice but then said 'I am not too sure about the eye; you make me look most peculiar.' Jim Callaghan seemed a bit concerned too – 'You've got it all wrong. You're simply not tall enough. Does my mouth really droop like that on one side?' I remember meeting Malcolm Muggeridge and telling him that to play him I simply put a lot of big words together, but I didn't really know what I was talking about. He just replied 'Neither do I, dear boy.'

Actually, I want them all to have long and successful careers. After all, my own living depends on it. For me, a general election is always a nightmare – look what happened just when I had Jim Callaghan going well!

I hope most viewers appreciate the spirit of what I am doing. I've had some fantastic audiences, but I think the best was on the last night of a six-day booking at a Caerphilly nightclub. At the end of the show everybody stood up and started singing 'We'll keep a welcome in the hillside . . . ' I remember too being really moved by an audience in a place called Irvine in Scotland. There had been few live shows there before and there must have been seventeen hundred people in the audience. But again it was the atmosphere and not the numbers that counted. I've had some disasters too, of course. The worst was at a private function in Liverpool. The whole audience consisted of people who were retiring from a large firm after twenty-five years of service. They had all been given clocks as commemorative gifts and they were sitting at tables with these clocks in front of them. I opened by asking if anyone could give me the right time, and the joke just died on me. I hadn't appreciated that they weren't exactly in a happy mood.

I spend so much time being other people that when I am at home I simply want to relax with my family and be myself. I am a family man at heart which is why I can enjoy laughter in the family. It's the best kind of laughter – and you should find plenty of it here. Have fun!

I

KIDS

I love kids and they seem to be quite fond of me too – they send about seventy per cent of my fan mail. Those that come up to me at the stage door often ask me to do an impression of Frank Spencer – then they do one too and they're often better than I am. That's life!

This section is dedicated to my own two: Charlotte, aged ten, and Clare, aged seven.

* * *

Timothy used to be the teacher's pet – she kept him in a cage in a corner of the classroom.

* * *

One small boy I know is called Six And Seven-Eighths – his parents picked his name out of a hat.

* * *

Our small daughter, Rosemary, was very quiet when our new neighbour called in for tea the other day. He asked why.

'Because,' said Rosemary, 'my mum gave me fifty pence if I promised not to say anything about your enormous nose and sticking-out ears.'

* * *

When the dentist asked Diana what filling she wanted for her teeth she replied: 'Strawberry.'

* * *

Teacher: 'What is a forum?'
Jenny: 'Please, Miss, isn't it a two-um plus a two-um?'

* * *

The last time my kids built a sandcastle on the beach a young man from the council arrived and gave them a rates demand.

* * *

Little Christina ran home and her mother asked her: 'Well, did you see if the butcher had pigs' feet?'

Christina replied: 'I don't know, mum, he had his shoes and socks on.'

* * *

The schoolteacher was asking her pupils what their ambitions were and she received various answers, ranging from 'being the first woman on the moon' to 'playing for a First Division football team.' But when she asked little Nigel what he most wanted to do he replied: 'Get my own back and wash behind my mother's ears.'

* * *

One boy I know was named after his father – they christened him Dad.

* * *

School doctor: 'Now, Sandra, do you have any trouble with your ears or nose?'
Sandra: 'Yes, sir. They get in the way when I take my jersey off.'

* * *

Teacher: 'Where are the Andes?'
Jonathan: 'At the end of my wristies.'

* * *

John: 'Can I share your sledge?'
Paul: 'Sure. We'll go halves.'
John: 'Fantastic!'
Paul: 'Yes – you can have it uphill and I'll have it downhill.'

* * *

My son is so tough he even makes the teacher stay in after school.

* * *

Mother: 'Have you changed the water in the goldfish bowl?'
Small boy (who obviously collected extremely ancient jokes): 'No, mum, they haven't drunk the last lot yet.'

* * *

Teacher: 'Now, Jimmy, what is next to cleanliness?'
Jimmy remained silent.
Teacher: 'Come, now, Jimmy. Surely you remember the proverb: "Cleanliness is next to . . . " '
Jimmy: 'Impossible.'

* * *

My friend christened her daughter Onyx – because she was onyx-pected.

* * *

Hazel and her parents had recently moved from Wales to England and it was Hazel's first day at her new school.

'Now, Hazel,' said the teacher, 'where do you come from?'

'Wales,' replied the girl.

'What part?'

'All of me, sir.'

* * *

Jenny, looking up from her homework: 'Oh, I wish I'd lived in olden times!'

Mother: 'Why, dear?'

Jenny: 'Because then I wouldn't have so much awful history to learn!'

* * *

I know what my sons are going to be when they grow up. They're going to be waiters. I know that because they never come when I call them.

* * *

Doctor: 'Now, Diane, I want you to take one of these pills twice a day.'

Diane: 'But how can I take it more than once?'

* * *

Father: 'Melanie, why do you keep scratching yourself?'

Melanie: 'Because I'm the only one who knows where I itch.'

* * *

'David! Stop that at once! How dare you throw the baby on the floor!'

'But mum, you said he was a bonny bouncing baby – I was only seeing how far he'd bounce . . . '

* * *

Teacher: 'Now, Gillian, if I had twenty apples in one hand and eighteen in the other hand, what would I have?'
Gillian: 'Very big hands, sir.'

* * *

When Timothy heard the TV weatherman say that tomorrow's weather would be 'rainy with patchy fog' he said to his mother: 'That's funny. I know we can have an Indian summer, but I didn't know there could be Apache fog.'

* * *

Father: 'Lesley, how many times do I have to tell you – stop eating off your knife.'
Lesley: 'But dad, my fork leaks.'

* * *

Teacher: 'Adrian, how do you spell "physical"?'
Adrian: 'F-i-z-z-i-c-a-l.'
Teacher: 'The dictionary gives the spelling as p-h-y-s-i-c-a-l.'
Adrian: 'But, sir, you didn't ask me how the dictionary spells it, you asked me how *I* spell it!'

* * *

'Simon, why are you pulling that piece of string behind you?'

'Have you ever tried to *push* a piece of string?'

* * *

Someone once said that adults consider the teens to be the most awkward age for their kids – too old to say anything cute, and too young to say anything sensible.

* * *

Out walking with her parents for her first holiday in the country, Joan suddenly stopped, looked into the village blacksmith's and yelled to her parents: 'Mum, dad, come quick! There's a man making a horse. He's nearly finished – he's just nailing on the back feet.'

* * *

At Sunday school the clergyman asked Lionel what he would do if he found a five-pound note lying on the ground outside the church on his way home.

'Would you keep it?' asked the clergyman.

'Of course not!'

'Good boy,' commented the clergyman. 'What would you do with it then?'

'Spend it,' responded Lionel.

* * *

When George was three years old he was such a terror that his parents, in utter desperation, pleaded with him to run away from home.

* * *

Susan carefully carried the brown paper bag into her classroom.

'What is in your bag?' asked her teacher.

'It's a present for you, sir,' replied Susan, holding out the bag.

'How nice! I wonder if I can guess what it is?'

The teacher touched the bottom of the bag. It was wet and sticky.

'Is it home-made jam?' he asked.

'No, sir.'

The teacher put his fingers on the bottom of the bag again and then licked his fingers.

'I know,' he said, 'it's home-made fudge.'

'Sorry, sir, but it's a little puppy.'

* * *

'How are you getting along with your arithmetic lessons?' Mrs Prendergasket asked her daughter.

'Oh, all right,' replied Helen.

'I see. Then you'll know what seven and two make,' said Mrs Prendergasket.

'No. We never learned that.'

'But surely you must know that seven and two make nine?'

'No, they don't,' said Helen. 'Teacher said today that five and four make nine.'

* * *

Dorothy: 'Mum, do all fairy stories start with "once upon a time"?'

Mother: 'No, dear. The ones your father tells start with "Sorry I'm late, but I was kept at the office." '

* * *

On my way home from work this evening I saw a small boy standing outside a door struggling to reach the knocker.

'Here, let me help you,' I said, knocking on the door loudly.

'Thanks, mister,' said the small boy, starting to run away. 'But don't stand there, you'll get caught.'

* * *

John got into terrible trouble when he went to the zoo. He said he was only feeding the penguins – which is true – but he was feeding them to the tigers.

* * *

It was Nigel's sixth birthday and he had received lots of very nice presents. He enjoyed playing with all the toys and games, but hated having to write all the 'thank you' letters to his various relatives.

'How many more letters do you have to write?' asked his mother, as he struggled with his pencil and paper.

'I'm doing the last one now.'

His mother looked at the letter. 'But why is your handwriting much larger in this one than in the others?'

'Because it's to grandma. She's deaf so I have to write loud.'

* * *

Kids ask such good questions nowadays. Why, only the other day my youngest son said: 'If Superman is so clever, how come he wears his underpants on top of his tights?'

* * *

Teacher: 'Lionel, if I gave you six bars of chocolate this morning and another seven bars this afternoon, how many bars of chocolate would you have?'

Lionel: 'Fifteen, miss.'

Teacher: 'But six bars plus seven bars only makes thirteen bars.'

Lionel: 'I know, miss. But I already had two bars of chocolate of my own before you started being so generous.'

* * *

Four-year-old Rebecca was looking at the cot in which her newly-arrived baby sister lay crying.

'Is it true that she came from Heaven?' asked Rebecca.

'Yes, dear,' replied her mother.

'Well,' commented Rebecca, 'if she made a noise like that up there it's no wonder they threw her out.'

* * *

Whenever any important guests come to dinner at our house I can always rely on my kids to be on their pest behaviour.

* * *

One morning the schoolteacher answered the telephone to hear a voice saying: 'I'm sorry to tell you that Carol won't be coming to school today – she's got a bad cold.'

'Oh,' said the teacher. 'I'm sorry to hear that. To whom am I speaking?'

'This,' said the voice, 'is my mother.'

* * *

Mother: 'Camilla, stop picking at your food! Why don't you eat your greens?'

Camilla: 'Because I don't like them, Mum.'

Mother: 'But they're very good for your skin – they'll help your complexion.'

Camilla: 'But I don't want to turn green!'

* * *

Geraldine: 'Did you know it's raining cats and dogs outside?'

Samantha: 'Yes. While I was out there I tripped and fell in a poodle.'

* * *

'Clarissa, why have you got that plate of tripe and onions on your head?'

'Because it's Thursday,' replied Clarissa.

'But today is Wednesday.'

'Oh,' said Clarissa, 'I feel such a fool.'

* * *

Gloria was born in such a poor neighbourhood that even the rainbows were black and white.

* * *

'Mum, now that I'm thirteen can I wear lipstick and make-up?'

'Certainly not, Claude!'

* * *

Father: 'Your mother said you only got one answer wrong in your maths exam today – is that true?'

Nigel: 'Yes, dad.'

Father: 'How many questions were there?'

Nigel: 'Thirty.'

Father: 'That's very good! So you got twenty-nine correct answers . . . '

Nigel: 'No, dad. Those were the questions I couldn't answer.'

* * *

The man took his very young son to the golf course to watch an important tournament.

They arrived just as one of the players was struggling with a ball and beating it in a bunker.

'Daddy,' asked the small boy, 'what does he do after he's killed it?'

* * *

Neighbour: 'And what's your baby sister's name?'
Andrea: 'I don't know. She can't talk properly yet.'

* * *

'Dad,' said the small girl, 'where did I come from?'

'Oh, the stork brought you.'

'And where did mummy come from?'

'The stork brought her, too,' replied the father.

'And what about you?'

'Oh,' chuckled her father, 'I was found under a gooseberry bush.'

It was this conversation that led to the little girl's essay at school stating: 'There have been no natural births in our family.'

* * *

'Now,' said Diana's mother, 'it's time for your piano lessons. Go and wash your hands and get ready.'

'Oh, mum,' sighed Diana, 'must I really go and wash? I promise I'll only use the black keys.'

* * *

Sandra's mother heard murmuring coming from inside Sandra's room so she quietly opened the door to find her daughter kneeling by the side of the bed and praying: 'Oh please, God, make the Andes be in India.'

'But Sandra, why do you want God to do that?' asked her mother.

'Because that's what I wrote in my geography test at school today.'

* * *

Miss Greenslade was Form 5A's new English teacher. She was in her early twenties and very attractive.

One day on entering her classroom she saw scrawled on the

blackboard: 'Richard Crunkle is the best kisser in town.' Annoyed, she ordered Richard to stay behind after the class had finished their lessons.

One hour after school had ended Richard's friends excitedly asked him how Miss Greenslade had punished him. Had he been given lines or extra homework?

Richard, who was rather conceited and very self-assured, simply smiled. 'It pays to advertise,' he said.

* * *

Grandmother: 'Susan, why are you staring at the grandfather clock like that?'
Susan: 'Well, I've seen the cuckoo pop out of the cuckoo clock, so now I'm waiting for grandfather to pop out of the grandfather clock.'

* * *

A cheeky young boy told the school doctor: 'Doctor, I've got a terrible complex. I keep thinking I'm a pack of cards.'

'Get to the back of the queue, then,' said the doctor, 'and I'll deal with you later.'

* * *

Sunday school teacher: 'Robin, what must we do in order to gain forgiveness for our sins?'
Robin: 'First we have to Sin.'

* * *

Miss Birtlebaum, the headmistress of a junior school, took fifty of her pupils to the big city so they could experience the delights of a real live opera.

The day started well, with all the kids enjoying the coach trip to the city, a picnic lunch in the park, and then the opera itself followed by tea with lots of cakes and ice cream.

'Well, did you enjoy the day?' asked Miss Birtlebaum.

'Yes, miss,' replied one of the older pupils. 'The picnic and the tea were smashing – and the coach ride was interesting. But that opera thing was a bit of a bore!'

* * *

Nigel came rushing home from school shouting: 'Dad, dad! I got a hundred in the exams.'

'Well done, son,' said the proud father.

'Yes,' continued Nigel, 'I got fifteen in maths, ten in science, twenty-five in geography, twenty in English, fifteen in history, and fifteen in art.'

* * *

Two very young boys were peering through a crack in the fence surrounding a nudist colony when one of their friends came up to them and asked: 'What are you doing?'

'Peering through a crack in the fence,' replied Sidney.

'What at?' asked the friend.

'I think they're called nudists,' said Clarence.

'Oh,' said the friend. 'Are they male or female?'

'I don't know,' replied Sidney. 'They haven't got any clothes on.'

* * *

Teacher: 'Jonathan, what is the outside of a tree trunk called?'
Jonathan: 'I don't know, sir.'
Teacher: 'Don't know? Don't know? Bark, boy! Bark, you stupid boy!'
Jonathan: 'Woof, woof!'

* * *

Mother: 'Darling, John had a terrible accident at school today.'
Father: 'What happened?'

Mother: 'It was during music lessons. Somehow he managed to swallow a mouth organ.'
Father: 'Well, look on the bright side – it's a good job he doesn't play a grand piano.'

* * *

Gloria was telling her friend how her family had just moved from a flat to a semi-detached house. 'And my bruvvers and me have each got our own room – we've lots more room now – but poor old mum still has to share a bedroom with dad.'

* * *

Simon was going to the Middle East for his holidays and so he had to have cholera and smallpox injections.

He bravely withstood the pain of the needles, but said: 'Please, miss, can you put the sticking plaster on my right arm?'

'But why?' asked the nurse. 'You had the injections in your left arm.'

'I know. But I have to go back to school this afternoon.'

'So?' queried the nurse. 'If you have the plaster over the injections on your left arm the other boys at school will realize you've had an injection and so won't bang against your arm.'

'You don't know the boys in my school!' commented Simon. '*That's* why I want the plaster on the wrong arm.'

* * *

Mr Gruntfirkin was sitting in the lounge reading a newspaper when he heard his son Robert thundering down the stairs in the hallway.

'Robert!' called Mr Gruntfirkin. 'Must you *always* come down the stairs sounding like a herd of elephants?'

'Sorry, dad.'

'You can just walk up them again now and then come down quietly.'

Robert went back up the stairs and Mr Gruntfirkin was

surprised when his son came down without making the usual terrible row.

'Why can't you always come down the stairs like that?' he asked.

'Sure, dad,' replied Robert. 'I'll always slide down the banisters in future.'

* * *

Adrian and Tony had just reached their eleventh birthdays and were having a general discussion about girls.

'There's this girl in our class with long yellowy hair and lots of freckles around her nose,' remarked Adrian.

'Yeah! I know who you mean. Fiona Logan.'

'That's her, yes. Fiona. Such a nice name.'

'And?' queried Tony.

'She lives quite near to me and every day I carry her books to and from school. And on Saturdays I take her to the cinema and buy her ice-creams and sweets, and on Sundays we go for walks in the park. I'm wondering if I ought to kiss her . . . '

'Of course not!' snorted Tony. 'You've done enough for her already.'

* * *

Mother: 'Julia, why are you crying?'
Julia: 'Because Sarah punched me.'
Mother: 'Where is Sarah? When did this happen?'
Julia: 'Sarah's gone home. She punched me about ten minutes ago.'
Mother: 'But I didn't hear you crying then.'
Julia: 'I wasn't. I thought you were out.'

* * *

A very posh couple had just moved into the area and were giving an 'open house' in order to get to know their neighbours.

Expensive wines were drunk; exotic foods were consumed;

and the chatter was terribly, terribly upper-middle-class.

Then right in the middle of the conversation the couple's four-year-old twins walked into the dining-room completely naked.

The conversation faltered for a few seconds. Hoping to overcome the situation, the parents of the twins started talking and soon everyone was chattering away again, completely ignoring the children who eventually walked out of the room.

Some minutes later, the mother went up to the twins' room: 'What have you just been doing?' she demanded.

'Oh, it's been very funny,' giggled one. 'We found some vanishing cream and smeared it all over ourselves and disappeared. We even went down to the dining-room and walked about – and no one even saw us!'

* * *

Maths teacher: 'Kirsty, if your mother borrows fifty pounds from me today and pays me back at the rate of one pound fifty pence per week, how much money will she still owe me in ten weeks' time?'
Kirsty: 'Fifty pounds, sir.'
Maths teacher: 'Surely not! If you think that you can't know much about simple arithmetic.'
Kirsty: 'But sir, you can't know much about my mother.'

* * *

2

BROTHERS

I don't have any real brothers – so I make do with the collection of assorted idiots to be found in the following pages.

* * *

At the age of six my brother ran away with a circus – but the police made him bring it back.

* * *

When he was twelve my brother bought an address book and labelled it: 'Girls – Volume One.'

* * *

Girls go out with my brother in dozens – they're afraid to go out with him alone.

* * *

My brother has just given up his latest beautiful girlfriend. He says he had to because she suddenly started using terrible four-letter words – like 'ring', 'baby' . . .

* * *

My brother Leonard used to work as a security guard at the docks. One day he was surprised to see one of the laziest dockers, Tom, trundling wheelbarrow loads of rubbish out of the dockyard.

His suspicions aroused, Leonard insisted on searching every load to see if Tom was trying to smuggle something out of the yard, but all the wheelbarrows contained was rubbish.

One week later Leonard lost his job – the police discovered that Tom had been stealing wheelbarrows!

* * *

My brother wants to be a doctor. He says it's the best job in the world – beautiful girls actually pay you to take all their clothes off and look at them.

* * *

I could always beat my brother with one hand – trouble is, I could never persuade him to fight with only one hand while I used two.

* * *

Last night my brother's girlfriend rang. As he was away, I asked her if she'd like to leave a message.

'Not really,' she said. 'But perhaps you can tell him I was thinking of him: 6 feet 2 inches in height, aged twenty-nine, pale complexion, blue eyes, shoulder-length dark brown hair, Roman nose, slim build and a birthmark on his left arm.'

I have a funny feeling that she might be a policewoman.

* * *

My journalist brother loved working for a Chinese newspaper in Hong Kong because it was one of the few places in the world where he could actually shout: 'Hold the back page!'

* * *

I told my brother that if he wanted to improve his eyesight he ought to eat more carrots.

'Like rabbits?' he asked.

'Yes,' I replied. 'You've never seen a rabbit wearing spectacles – so carrots must be good for the eyesight.'

After following my advice for some months my brother was able to spot a thimble from 300 yards away – trouble is, he keeps tripping over his ears.

* * *

My brother used to be a comedian but he was so bad that the clubs where he performed charged 50 pence to get in and £2 to get out.

* * *

My brother Lionel is a very efficient businessman. Everything in his office is neatly catalogued and filed – documents can be found instantly and his card index system is infallible.

Last week when he went on a business trip to Hamburg he sent his wife a neatly typed card which read: 'Having a wonderful time. Wish you were her.' At the top was his secretary's reference mark.

* * *

'Doctor, I'm a bit worried about my younger brother.'

'Why, what's wrong with him?'

'Well, he loves climbing trees.'

'So do most boys.'

'And he's built himself a tree-house and spends nearly all his time in it.'

'So – he just seems like a normal healthy boy.'

'Yes, but he wants his wife and kids to live in the tree-house, too.'

* * *

My brother says he would prefer not to take his girlfriend out and do things – he wants to take her in and undo things.

* * *

My brother went to a terrible boarding house in Weymouth for his holiday. On the first morning of his stay he was woken at 7 a.m.

'Why did you wake me up?' he asked the proprietor of the boarding house. 'I thought you served breakfast at 8 a.m.'

'So we do,' replied the proprietor. 'But you have to get up at 7 a.m. to give us time to take the sheets off your bed.'

'Couldn't that wait until after breakfast?'

'No,' said the proprietor. 'We need the sheets for tablecloths.'

* * *

My brother is so conceited I once heard him tell a girl: 'Darling, sometimes you make me wish I had a much lower IQ so that I could really enjoy your company.'

* * *

My brother Nicholas insists on wearing a pork pie hat – even though the gravy keeps running down the back of his neck.

* * *

The reason my brother didn't do very well at university is that every evening he used to toss a coin: if it came down heads he'd go out drinking with his friends, if it was tails he'd go and visit his girlfriend in her flat – and if the coin stood on its edge he'd stay in his room and study.

* * *

I was in a restaurant with my brother last night and he was very attracted to a beautiful young lady who was sitting alone at another table.

Sitting down opposite her, he said: 'I found you so dazzlingly beautiful that I had to come over, so I can gaze into your flawless face, superbly framed by your adorable, silky, long blonde hair. I was filled with an irresistible desire to present you with a mink coat to wrap around your slim, elegant figure; I wanted to adorn your fingers with diamonds; and give you whatever your heart may desire.'

'Ooh!' said the girl, somewhat overcome.

'Will you come home with me and allow me to discover your every little wish?'

'Oh, yes,' sighed the girl. 'I'd love to see your home. Do you have a mansion, a penthouse flat . . . '

'No,' said my brother. 'I live above the fish and chip shop round the corner.'

* * *

My brother went to the doctor because he kept forgetting things (even terrible old jokes).

'How long have you had this problem?' asked the doctor.

'What problem?' asked my brother.

* * *

After my brother had been going out with Janice Montgomery-Blibbingbladder for some months, her father said to him: 'I'd like a quiet word with you, old chap.'

'What about?' asked my brother.

'Oh, just general things, you know. But one thing in particular, if you don't mind me raising the subject . . . are your intentions towards my daughter honourable or dishonourable?'

'Well,' said my brother, 'it's jolly decent of you to give me a choice . . . '

* * *

When my brother was on holiday last year he stayed in a small guesthouse where the owner said: 'My terms for bed and breakfast are £5 a night – but if you make your own bed it's half-price.'

'Then I'll make my own bed,' replied my brother.

The guesthouse owner then gave him a hammer, some nails and several planks of wood.

* * *

My eldest brother has been engaged to the same lady for forty-six years.

'Isn't it about time you got married?' I asked him.

'Yes,' he replied. 'But who would have me now?'

* * *

My brother used to be a comedian, and he decided to get a top agent to represent him. As top agents don't agree to represent just anyone, my brother had to audition.

'There was this Chinese . . . ' began my brother.

'Stop!' said the agent. 'Jokes about the Chinese don't go down too well – besides, Britain is friendly with China.'

'Oh. There was this Italian . . . '

The agent shook his head.

'A Jew went to . . . '

'Too many Jewish jokes already,' said the agent. 'And they're much better told by Jews – and you are not Jewish.'

'There was this Irishman . . . '

'Stop! You really want me to represent you? If so, be different. Everyone tells jokes about the Irish. Anyone who can do a whole act without mentioning an Irishman shows he has class . . . '

'What about South Africans?'

'OK. You can make jokes about them. They have learned how to be thick-skinned.'

'Good!' said my brother. 'This South African, Wong Ping-

Lin, was eating spaghetti outside a synagogue in Dublin when . . . '

* * *

On his first day at work as a salesman my brother got two orders from people he called on. One was 'Get out' and the other was 'Go away.'

* * *

My brother Tom went on a 'singles only' holiday to Sardinia where he met and fell in love with a girl named Flora.

All went well for the first week – he wined and dined her at the most expensive restaurants, bought her beautiful gowns, and gave her diamond-studded jewellery.

She said she loved him – and he expressed his love for her by writing romantic poetry which he sent to her with little gifts of furs, perfumes and orchids.

Then suddenly she said she couldn't see him ever again. 'But why?' he asked, and she refused to answer, until one day he found her wrapped in the embrace of a middle-aged man on the beach. He demanded to know what was going on. 'You said you loved me to the very last,' he said.

'I know, and I did,' replied the girl. 'But you soon spent all your money – it didn't last long.'

* * *

'I've been very impressed with your work,' said my brother's boss, 'and we've decided to make you a director of the company.'

'Thanks, Mr Pushpull,' said my brother.

'And now you're on the board,' continued Mr Pushpull, 'you don't need to use my surname any more – just call me Boss.'

* * *

3

SISTERS

I'm only related to one sister, but I seem to have collected a lot of others – sisters of the characters I impersonate. I had a letter once from Robin Day's sister. This section is dedicated to my real sister, Josephine, with the promise that she won't find any jokes about Napoleon here!

* * *

My sister insists on wearing very revealing dresses. I don't know if she's deliberately trying to catch a cold – or catch a man.

* * *

My sister came home the other day and said she'd been sacked from her job.

'What for?' I asked.

'Well, you know I work for an estate agent?'

'Yes.'

'I've been sacked for honesty.'

* * *

My sister went to the doctor recently about her terrible problem.

'Doctor,' she said, 'whenever I see a man put on a pair of spectacles I get an overwhelming urge to kiss him. Can you do anything for me?'

'Yes,' replied the doctor. 'Stay there while I go and fetch my glasses from my bag.'

* * *

When my sister was a nurse everyone used to call her Appendix – because all the doctors wanted to take her out.

* * *

I think my sister is money-mad: she doesn't have any money, and that's probably why she's mad.

* * *

My sister is looking for a man who will look up to her. I think that explains why she keeps going out with midgets.

* * *

I once took my sister to a river bank for a picnic. It was a very hot day so I asked if she felt like going for a swim.

'Don't be silly – the water isn't deep enough.'

'Of course it is!' I replied.

'No it isn't,' she insisted. 'Just look at those ducks.'

I looked. 'Well?'

'The water only comes half-way up their bodies!'

* * *

Yesterday my sister came home looking very happy.

'You look very pleased with yourself,' I said.

'Yes,' she replied. 'My boss has just given me the most beautiful musquash coat.'

'To keep you warm?'

'No. To keep me quiet.'

* * *

My sister went on a reducing diet last week – now she's disappeared.

* * *

My sister went to buy some fly spray, but there were so many different types available in the supermarket that she decided to ask for help.

'Is this spray any good for flies?' she asked one of the assistants, holding out a can.

'Not really,' replied the assistant. 'It kills them.'

* * *

My sister says she'll go through anything for a man – like his jacket and trouser pockets, wallet, bank balance . . .

* * *

My sister is a bit crazy about boys. The other day she even went to her optician and asked if he could give her a pair of boy-focal spectacles.

* * *

After she had been married for a month I asked my sister what she thought of married life.

'Oh, it's fantastic!' she replied. 'It's almost like being in love.'

* * *

When my sister was a trainee nurse a doctor asked her if she had taken a patient's temperature.

She replied: 'No. If it's missing it wasn't me who took it.'

* * *

My sister says her boss keeps complaining about the rent he's paying. I asked her what that's got to do with her – and she replied: 'It's my rent he's paying.'

* * *

Last week my sister and I went to a party where she met David. I thought she seemed very flattered by his attentions and it looked as if their relationship might develop further. Unfortunately, my sister is a bit scatterbrained:
David: 'It's been great meeting you. Really great. Perhaps we can meet again? Tomorrow? For dinner?'
My sister: 'Lovely!'
David: 'What's your phone number, so I can get in touch?'
My sister: 'It's in the phone book.'
David: 'But I don't know your last name.'
My sister: 'That's in the phone book too.'

* * *

When my sister was being courted by a doctor she had to take his love letters to the chemist in order to find out what he'd written.

* * *

My sister likes to bring out the animal in men – like mink, musquash, fox . . .

* * *

I once heard my sister ask her boyfriend whether she should wear her old woollen dress or her new cotton one. He replied: 'It doesn't matter, darling – you know I'll always love you through thick or thin.'

* * *

Nigel: 'I don't know what to get for my sister's birthday.'
Simon: 'How old will she be?'
Nigel: 'Fifteen.'
Simon: 'Ah! Then I know just what she'll want most.'
Nigel: 'What's that?'
Simon: 'A sixteen-year-old boy.'

* * *

My sister did extremely well in her cookery examination – she told me she got 100 out of 100 for defrosting.

* * *

My sister went to a party and during the last dance a handsome young man asked her: 'May I take you home?'

'Of course,' replied my sister. 'Where do you live?'

* * *

My mother came home late one night to find my sister sitting on the sofa with her boyfriend.

'Get out!' shrieked my mother at the boy. 'Get out! You're nothing but an uncouth rogue. I thought I told you never to see my daughter again.'

'I know,' replied the boy. 'That's why we turned the lights out.'

* * *

My sister's favourite dresses are the ones that bring out the bust in her.

* * *

4

HUSBANDS

I'm going to dedicate this chapter to myself, as I've been a husband for eleven years. Some of these jokes are told from experience – but I'm not going to tell you which ones, or I might end up being an ex-husband!

* * *

My husband is so fat that the last time he stood on a speak-your-weight machine at the seaside the machine said: 'No coach parties please.'

* * *

My husband says he is going to go on a diet as he wants to get back to his former slim, handsome self. Personally, I think he is just a wishful shrinker.

* * *

The solicitor's door was flung open and an angry husband walked in.

'I want a divorce!' demanded the man.

'Please sit down,' said the solicitor.

'I want a divorce!' repeated the man.

'I know. Just calm yourself and I'll see what I can do. It isn't that simple to get a divorce – there have to be sufficient grounds.'

'I've got ample grounds for divorce,' retorted the man.
'Such as?'
'My wife said I was not a very good lover.'
'So?' queried the solicitor.
'How does she know the difference?'

* * *

My husband is so stupid that when I gave birth to triplets he wanted to know who the fathers of the other two were.

* * *

The hard-working husband had been on a two-month sales trip overseas, visiting forty-three towns in six different countries. Yet not once had he strayed – his thoughts had always been on his wife.

Now, at the end of his journey, he was looking forward to holding her in his arms again: he had missed her terribly for she was the one and only love of his life.

As he opened his front door and went into the lounge he saw his wife sitting in an armchair watching television.

'I'm home, darling!' he called. 'Did you miss me while I was away?'

'Oh!' said his wife, her eyes still fixed on the small screen, 'Have you been away?'

* * *

The only thing my husband finds hard to give is in.

* * *

Mrs Greenglobal: 'My, it's good to see you again. Has your husband still got his terrible cold?'
Mrs Birdtwit: 'Yes, I'm afraid so.'
Mrs Greenglobal: 'But is it getting any better?'
Mrs Birdtwit: 'Well, you know him. When he's getting better

he growls and grumbles so much that sometimes I think it's better when he's worse.'

* * *

It was 2 a.m. and Mrs Jenkins woke up, turned on the bedside lamp and nudged her husband.

'John! Wake up!'

'Urrr . . . errrr . . . ' he mumbled.

'Get up! Get up!' said Mrs Jenkins, poking him in the ribs.

'What is it?'

'I can hear noises downstairs.'

'So what?' he muttered. 'It's probably the cat.'

'No. It's burglars. I can hear them walking about in the kitchen. You know I've always had very sensitive hearing . . . '

'Yes,' commented Mr Jenkins. 'You're the only woman I know who can hear dog whistles.'

'So if I say I can hear burglars, I can hear burglars,' insisted Mrs Jenkins.

'What do you want me to do? Go down there and get beaten up? The phone's in the hall and they'll hear me if I go downstairs and try to call the police.'

'Shush!' whispered Mrs Jenkins. 'They've stopped walking about. Oh, I do hope they're not going to come upstairs – I've still got my curlers in. Ah! I can hear them opening the fridge.'

'Maybe they think we keep our money in there?' suggested the husband. 'Keeping it on ice.'

'No, I think they're eating the rock cakes I made for the party tomorrow.'

'Oh!'

'Yes, they're definitely eating the rock cakes – I can hear them munching.'

'Oh well then,' said Mr Jenkins, turning over ready to go to sleep again, 'That solves the problem. If they're eating your rock cakes I can go down tomorrow morning and bury them.'

* * *

My husband arrived home unexpectedly early yesterday evening and found me with a naked man.

It shows you how stupid he is – he even believed my story that the man was a nudist who had come in to use the telephone.

* * *

Alice: 'Doctor, my husband is driving me crazy.'
Doctor: 'How?'
Alice: 'He thinks he's a refrigerator.'
Doctor: 'So what's bad about that? He'll probably thaw out of it eventually. You mustn't let yourself be worried by small complexes like that.'
Alice: 'But you must *do* something! It stops me sleeping at night.'
Doctor: 'Oh, how?'
Alice: 'Well, he lies on his back snoring and when he's got his mouth open the little light inside wakes me up.'

* * *

When I told my husband that the local psychiatrist had arranged a series of meetings for schizophrenics he said that he had half a mind to go.

* * *

My husband has just made it into the Top Twenty – the Top Twenty List Of Failures.

* * *

When I married my husband he made me a woman whose name is on the tip of everyone's tongue – I stopped being Miss Janice Gruntbirtle and became Mrs Spit.

* * *

Someone once defined a husband as being the person who, while on holiday with his wife, holds open the car door while she takes out the suitcases and carries them into the hotel.

* * *

Any get-up-and-go which my husband had soon got-up-and-went after I married him.

* * *

My husband normally drives a car – but when it had to go in for servicing he was forced to take several buses in order to get to work.

When the ticket inspector approached him on the top deck of the bus and asked him 'Where did you get on?', my husband replied: 'Downstairs.'

* * *

I can still remember the day my husband proposed to me. He said: 'Darling, I know I'm not very handsome, rich or clever, but will you marry me?'

I said: 'Of course. And it doesn't matter about not being handsome – you'll be out at work all day and you can always get a second job at night to earn some extra money.'

* * *

Business is so slow in my husband's office that he doesn't watch the clock – he watches the calendar.

* * *

I wouldn't say that my husband has lost interest in me, but one of our recent conversations went something like this:
Me: 'I'm home, darling.'

Husband, looking up from newspaper: 'Oh. Yes. Welcome back, darling.'
Me: 'Notice anything different?'
Husband: 'So you've been buying things in the sales again?'
Me: 'I'm afraid so. Can you guess what?'
Husband: 'New handbag?'
Me: 'No.'
Husband: 'More jewellery to add to your enormous collection?'
Me: 'No.'
Husband: 'It's not something big, like a new car or a mink coat, is it?'
Me: 'No.'
Husband: 'Are you wearing it?'
Me: 'Yes.'
Husband: 'Ah! I've got it! I did think you were looking a bit different. You're wearing a new dress.'
Me: 'No.'
Husband: 'Oh. It looked quite new. Maybe you haven't worn it very often. Is it new shoes?'
Me: 'No.'
Husband: 'And you say you're wearing it. I can't guess what it is – I give up.'
Me: 'I went to a jumble sale and I'm wearing a secondhand gas mask.'

* * *

When my husband was promoted he thought it would be good for his image if he took up golf.

He bought all the best golfing instruction books, purchased an expensive set of clubs, and within a few weeks he felt ready to face the challenge of a major golf course.

After his first morning on the green he came home smiling and happy.

'Did you do well?' I asked.

'Fantastic!' he replied. 'It only took me sixty-eight strokes.'

'That's good.'

'Yes,' he said, 'and tomorrow I'm going to see how many it takes me to get the second hole.'

* * *

My husband is very versatile – he can do anything wrong.

* * *

My husband decided to change his job and so he went to a careers adviser to take an aptitude test to see what he was most suitable for. The results showed that he was only suitable for retirement.

* * *

Mrs Pogglethwaite: 'My husband always takes me to the best restaurants.'
Mrs Greenburger: 'That's nice.'
Mrs Pogglethwaite: 'Yes. Maybe one day he might even take me *in*.'

* * *

Mrs Gruntlow is on the telephone: 'Hello? This is Mrs Gruntlow. Is that the cricket club?'

'Yes,' replies the voice on the phone.

'Is my husband there?'

'Yes.'

'Can I speak to him?'

'I'm sorry, but he's just going in to bat.'

'Oh,' says Mrs Gruntlow. 'Then I'll hold on – I'm sure he won't be very long.'

* * *

My husband thought he had an inferiority complex so he went to a psychiatrist. After many months of consultations the chiatrist told him what I've known for years – he doesn't have an inferiority complex: he really is inferior.

* * *

My husband is extremely forgetful. If I didn't watch him closely he'd probably go to work in his pyjamas.

The other day I phoned him at work to remind him that we were entertaining his boss to dinner in our home that evening.

My husband said: 'I know. But what's the address?'

* * *

I never have a battle of wits with my husband – it wouldn't be fair as he's only half-armed.

* * *

I can't remember when my husband's birthday is – but I think it's sometime this year.

* * *

My husband has become a golf fanatic. The other day I went to meet him at the golf club and arrived just as he was walking into the clubhouse with his partner slung over his shoulder.

'What's happened to Sidney?' I asked.

'He collapsed. I tried to revive him, but he died.'

'How awful!' I said.

'Yes. Absolutely dreadful. Took me much longer to go round the course than usual. Ever since the fifth hole I've had to put him down, take a swing, pick him up, walk to the ball, put him down, take a swing, pick him up . . . '

* * *

My husband likes to support sick animals – the trouble is, he is not aware that they are sick when he backs them.

*   *   *

5

WIVES

Groucho Marx said that behind every successful man stands a woman, and behind her stands his wife. However, I think it is true that wives help their husbands to success – it certainly has been in the case of Sandra and me. This chapter is, of course, dedicated to her.

* * *

When my wife was asked what she and I had in common she replied: 'Well, we were both married on the same day.'

* * *

Before we were married my wife went to evening classes to study cookery. Judging from the results ever since I think the course must have been advertised as 'Simple Cookery In Twenty Greasy Lessons.'

* * *

When my wife was in hospital and was asked if she wanted a bed-pan she replied: 'You mean I have to do my own cooking in bed?'

* * *

It was my wife's birthday and she said to me: 'Darling, I hope you haven't bought me a big, expensive present?'

'Why?' I asked.

'Because yesterday I saw something absolutely wonderful so I went and bought it.'

'Where is it?' I asked.

'Oh, it's not here yet. The shop is delivering it this afternoon.'

'What is it?'

'Now, dear, don't be silly! I can't tell you what it is – I want it to be a surprise.'

* * *

My wife always lets me have a voice in what she buys – the invoice.

* * *

I was in my club the other day when I heard a man say: 'You know, English women are the best in the world. You just can't beat them.'

'Rubbish!' snorted his companion. 'I beat mine every day.'

* * *

When my wife gave birth to our first son we had differences of opinion as to what to christen him.

'Let's call him Nigel,' I suggested.

'Don't be stupid!' my wife replied. 'Every Tom, Dick and Harry is called Nigel nowadays.'

* * *

Two men were talking in a bar:
Andrew: 'My wife spends so much money that I'm thinking of giving her plastic surgery.'

Derek: 'But how can surgery stop her spending money?'
Andrew: 'I'll cut off her plastic credit card.'

* * *

My wife and I went to Blackpool recently and our hotel room was immediately above the kitchens.

'Good grief!' I cried, swatting at one of the enormous bluebottles that was flying around the room. 'The flies are really thick in here.'

'What do you expect in Blackpool,' said my wife, 'educated ones?'

* * *

Soon after we were married my wife cooked me a large steak for dinner – but it had a very odd taste.

'Darling, what seasonings or spices did you use on the steak?' I asked.

'Oh. I didn't use any. Was I supposed to?' replied my wife.

'No, dear. But the steak tastes a bit funny.'

'Oh! I hope it's not because I put too much sunburn cream on it.'

'Sunburn cream!' I spluttered, spitting out bits of meat. 'What did you put sunburn cream on it for?'

'Well,' replied my wife demurely, 'I burnt the steak, so I thought sunburn cream would make it pink and tender again.'

* * *

My wife believes that most people can keep a secret – it's the people they tell them to who can't.

* * *

I gave my wife a carving set for her birthday: two chisels, a hammer, and a circular saw.

* * *

Before I married my wife I thought she was like a bird in a gilded cage – now I know the truth: she's a bulge in a girdled cage.

* * *

Simon: 'Doctor, as a medical man and a friend, I hope you can help me.'
Doctor: 'Sure, Simon. You know if you ever need help you only have to ask. What's the trouble?'
Simon: 'It's my wife.'
Doctor: 'Your wife? But she's beautiful, witty, and seems in perfect health . . .'
Simon: 'She's got sinus trouble.'
Doctor: 'Sinus trouble?'
Simon: 'Yes. Every day it's "sign us a cheque, sign us a cheque."'

* * *

I took my wife to the National Gallery the other day, but she was rather bored until she came to one of the landscapes and said: 'Huh! I don't know why they hang that in here!'

'Why do you say that?' I asked.

'I thought you said they only have important pictures in the National Gallery?'

'They do.'

'Then why do they show that? It's the same as the picture on last year's calendar!'

* * *

The last time my wife agreed with me was when she said 'I do' at our wedding.

* * *

My wife keeps saying she's made many sacrifices to me – I think she must be referring to the burnt offerings she gives me at mealtimes.

* * *

Gloria: 'Janice! How good to see you after all these years.'
Janice: 'And you, too, Gloria. I hear you've just got married.'
Gloria: 'That's right. And there's only one thing stopping me from being a happily married woman.'
Janice: 'And what's that?'
Gloria: 'My husband.'

* * *

My wife's cooking is so bad she's even given the dustbin ulcers.

* * *

The other day my wife cooked a cottage pie. Five minutes later three men from the council came in and condemned it.

* * *

'I'm fed up with wearing this old fox coat,' said my wife. 'Surely you can't expect me to wear this tatty old thing all my life?'

'Why not?' I asked sweetly. 'The fox did.'

* * *

My wife still ruins my cornflakes for breakfast. She will insist on trying to boil them in the packet.

* * *

My wife crept out of bed late last night as she was worried about our daughter, who was still sitting in the lounge with her boyfriend.

When she opened the lounge door she discovered our daughter in the middle of a passionate kissing session.

'Stop it! Stop it!' screamed my wife. 'You said I could trust you to behave yourself – so how is it I find you kissing and cuddling like that? How is it?'

'Fantastic!' murmured our daughter.

* * *

Fed up with being a golf widow, Mrs Pushley insisted on accompanying her husband on his latest trip to the golf club.

'You can teach me how to play,' she said. 'And then I can be your regular partner.'

Mr Pushley was not very keen on the idea – even less so when she proved she was a much better player than he was: she scored a hole in one with her very first shot.

Walking up to the ball in the hole, Mrs Pushley asked her husband: 'Now, how do I hit it out of this little hole?'

* * *

The only kisses I get from my wife are rainbow kisses – they only come after a storm.

* * *

6

MOTHERS-IN-LAW

I don't usually do mother-in-law jokes – I leave that to Les Dawson. He once met my mother-in-law and was very nice to her, though I don't know what he's like to his own. Actually I feel a bit sorry for mothers-in-law, so I hope all these jokes will make them laugh, too, because, as we all know, most of them aren't a bit like the ones we make jokes about. My own mother-in-law, Alma, certainly isn't – and this chapter is dedicated to her.

* * *

My mother-in-law reminds me of the Mona Lisa – her face is flat, stretched and oily.

* * *

Last Sunday we went round to my mother-in-law's place for tea. It was quite enjoyable, especially the rock cakes – I helped her build a rockery with them.

* * *

I wouldn't say that my mother-in-law is silly, but the other day she went to a secondhand shop and asked them to fix one on her watch.

* * *

The other week my mother-in-law went window shopping – and came home with sixteen windows.

* * *

My mother-in-law thinks she knows it all. The other day we were walking in the High Street and I heard a terrible noise.

'I think someone's screaming in agony,' I said.

'Oh, that's all right,' replied my mother-in-law, 'I speak it fluently.'

* * *

My mother-in-law has everything a man could possibly want – huge muscles, a hairy chest and a large moustache.

* * *

My mother-in-law has been ugly all her life. When she was a baby and her parents took her to be christened, the clergyman took one look, laughed and said: 'What a good joke! Now take this baboon away and fetch the baby.'

* * *

My mother-in-law is always complaining. She's even complained in a restaurant that the ice-cream was too cold.

The other day I took her to a very expensive restaurant and we had just started on the soup when she called over the head waiter.

'Waiter!' she said. 'This soup is disgusting. Foul! Absolutely foul! It isn't fit for a pig.'

'I'm sorry, madam,' said the waiter, who was used to her tantrums. 'I'll go and get some which is.'

* * *

This morning my mother-in-law came down to breakfast and said: 'Oh dear! I'm not myself today.'

'Yes,' I replied. 'I did notice the improvement.'

* * *

My mother-in-law is so huge she was born on September 5th, 6th, 7th, 8th and 9th.

* * *

When my mother-in-law goes on holiday she always returns with a sunburnt tongue.

* * *

It was my mother-in-law's birthday yesterday. I bought her a lovely chair – but she refuses to let me plug it in.

* * *

Whenever I visit my mother-in-law she always gives me enthusiasm soup – she puts everything she's got into it.

* * *

My mother-in-law is always speaking through her nose – she's worn her mouth out.

* * *

My mother-in-law is always boasting about her looks. She even claims that when she was a little girl she won an 'adorable girl of the year' award and was presented with a silver cup by the prime minister. But I don't believe her story. I'm sure William Pitt never gave out cups for that sort of thing.

* * *

My mother-in-law was washing up the dishes while I wiped them. Each time she took a dish out of the water she dried her hands. I asked her why.

'Because my doctor makes me take a lot of iron tablets and I don't want to go rusty.'

* * *

My mother-in-law recently spent several hundred pounds on a new facial treatment. Now she looks a million – a million years old.

* * *

I recently discovered how to stop the very irritating knocking noises in my car: I made my mother-in-law travel by bus.

* * *

My mother-in-law can talk ninety per cent faster than anyone can listen.

* * *

The other day I was waiting outside a phone box when I realized that my mother-in-law was in it.

I had a very urgent phone call to make, but inside the box my mother-in-law was just flipping through the telephone directories in a leisurely fashion.

I waited patiently for ten minutes – but still she continued looking through the phone books without making a call.

I opened the door. 'Can I help you?' I asked. 'Whose telephone number are you looking for?'

'Oh!' said my mother-in-law. 'I'm not looking for a number – I'm just looking for a nice name for your baby daughter.'

* * *

My mother-in-law won the 'Best Dressed Woman Of 1901' award – in 1980.

* * *

My mother-in-law recently went to the doctor and said: 'Doctor, can you help me? I keep losing my temper.'

'I beg your pardon?' said the doctor.

'I just told you once,' she retorted, 'you stupid old idiot!'

* * *

My mother-in-law recently invested all her life-savings in a newspaper shop – but it blew away.

* * *

When my mother-in-law's car refused to start she towed it to the garage (she's a very large, strong lady).

'What's the matter with it?' she demanded.

The garage mechanic looked at the car, opened the bonnet, poked around a bit, and said: 'It's obvious, madam. The battery is flat.'

'Then what shape should it be?' she demanded.

* * *

My mother-in-law is so powerfully built that when she went shoplifting she managed to lift up two supermarkets, a delicatessen, and the local fish and chip shop.

* * *

The hotel owner, keen to increase trade in winter, decided to hold a conference especially for mothers-in-law.

The conference was a great success and the hotel owner was interviewed by the local television station about it.

'This must surely be a unique conference,' said the television presenter. 'A conference aimed solely at mothers-in-law – and you managed to attract 144 of them to it. But how would you yourself describe such a gathering?'

'Bearing in mind the numbers,' said the hotel owner, 'it could only be called gross stupidity.'

* * *

When I told my mother-in-law that her soup tasted like dish-water she said: 'How do you know?'

* * *

7

FATHERS-IN-LAW

There aren't many father-in-law jokes – perhaps because there aren't many women comedians. My own father-in-law, Eric, used to be a musician, and he's certainly told me a thing or two about show business. This chapter is dedicated to him, with the promise that the fathers-in-law in these jokes are not in any way modelled on him!

* * *

My father-in-law is a real success story. When he started in business he only had £10,000 – now he owes £ ½ million.

* * *

My father-in-law is such an optimist that if he fell down a lift shaft he'd swear he was going up.

* * *

Sometimes I think my father-in-law is slightly eccentric. The other night he went to bed with a tape measure saying he wanted to find out how long he slept.

* * *

My father-in-law decided to give up smoking, so he went his doctor to ask for advice.

'Whenever you feel like a cigarette,' said the doctor, 'put a carrot in your mouth.'

The problem is, the carrot won't stay alight.

* * *

My father-in-law is a man of rare gifts – I've been married to his daughter for twenty-nine years and he's never given me a present.

* * *

When my father-in-law was on holiday he met a clairvoyant.

'Nice weather we're having today,' commented my father-in-law.

'Yes,' replied the clairvoyant, 'it makes me think of the lovely summer we'll have in 1987.'

* * *

My father-in-law believes that we should do all we can to preserve wild life. He makes his contribution by pickling rabbits.

* * *

When my father-in-law went to the mind-reader she said there was so little to read that she'd only charge him half price.

* * *

All the people in my father-in-law's office call him Myriapod. This is because the word 'Myriapod' describes creatures like centipedes and millipedes – creatures who, like him, got where they are today by crawling.

* * *

My father-in-law is so mean that the other day I found him crying, even though he'd just won a fantastic holiday for two in a raffle.

'Surely you should be crying with happiness,' I said, 'to have such good luck.'

'Good luck?' he replied. 'But I bought three raffle tickets and the other two didn't win anything!'

* * *

Last year I went to spend a brief holiday with my father-in-law, who lives in Arizona, right in the middle of the desert.

No matter how hard I tried, I couldn't fall asleep – the noise of all the desert creatures kept me awake.

'Why do the coyotes howl all the time?' I asked my father-in-law.

'Well,' he said, 'coyotes are like large dogs, and as there aren't many trees around here – they have to make do with cactus.'

* * *

My father-in-law is a politician. My wife insisted that I went to hear him speak during an election campaign.

I found it all extremely tedious. He ranted on and on: 'What this country wants is total reform!' he cried. 'Give me Common Market reform! What I want is farm subsidy reform! Electoral reform! Monetary reform! Social reform!'

I couldn't resist shouting from the back of the hall: 'And chloroform!'

* * *

My father-in-law has joined twenty different unions – that way, he hopes, there's a chance that he'll always be on strike.

* * *

My father-in-law asked me if I'd like to accompany him on safari – but I had to confess: 'I've never played it before. Do you have the piano music?'

* * *

'How is married life?' asked my father-in-law.

'All right,' I replied. 'Except for your daughter. I've been married to her for a month and all she can do is nag and nag. She can't cook, insists on wearing the most dreadful clothes, and her main aim in life seems to be to get as fat as possible. Is there any chance you might take her back?'

'Certainly not! You married her for better or for worse.'

'I know,' I said. 'I seem to have got her for worse.'

* * *

'I met a woman in the pub the other day,' said my father-in-law, 'and she was trying to buy a drink with some strange-looking money.'

'Counterfeit?' I asked.

'Yes. She had two.'

* * *

My father-in-law went to the doctor and said: 'Doctor, please can you help me. I feel really awful. I'm sure you can help me out.'

'Certainly, sir,' said the doctor, and showed him the door.

* * *

My father-in-law believes in the motto: 'Blessed are the pure, for they shall inhibit the earth.'

* * *

My father-in-law's front teeth are so large that he's the only man I know who can lie on the beach and prop himself up without using his arms.

* * *

My father-in-law has absolutely no sense of humour. Even if you told him a joke with a double-meaning, he wouldn't get either of them.

* * *

8

GRANDPARENTS

My mother's parents come from Ireland where my grandad used to take me to the pub – even though I was only eight years old at the time and drank lemonade! I hope that I'm around long enough to take my own grandchildren out, too. Sandra's grandmother is still alive, so our kids have a great-grandmother. She's a grand old lady and enjoys having a good laugh with us.

I've dedicated this chapter to Sandra and me in the year 2000, by which time we'll probably qualify for it.

* * *

My grandfather was taking a short cut through the cemetery when it suddenly started to rain. Sheltering under a tree, he met the cemetery gardener.

'Terrible weather we're having,' commented grandfather.

'Aye,' agreed the gardener, 'but this is only a shower – and the ground needs the rain. This is sure to bring things up.'

'I sincerely hope not,' replied my grandfather. 'I've got two wives buried in here.'

* * *

On reaching the age of 100, my grandfather was interviewed by a reporter from the local newspaper.

'And you say you haven't an enemy in the world – despite living so long?' said the reporter, who knew of grandfather's long business career in which he had out-cheated a large number of people.

'True,' replied grandfather. 'Not one enemy in the entire world.' He grinned widely: 'I've outlived them all!'

* * *

My grandfather is so old he says he can remember when Madame Butterfly was only a caterpillar.

* * *

Grandfather: 'Doctor, what would you say if I told you I was getting married again?'
Doctor: 'Congratulations. You're not too old at ninety-three to experience the joys of marriage again and I'm sure the companionship will do you a world of good.'
Grandfather: 'That's what I thought.'
Doctor: 'And where did you meet your future bride-to-be – at the Old Folks' Club?'
Grandfather: 'Oh, no! She's only twenty-three.'
Doctor: 'Twenty-three! This puts a very different light on things . . . you know this could prove fatal?'
Grandfather: 'Well, if she dies I suppose I'm not too old to find another . . .'

* * *

My grandfather was being interviewed by the local television station:

Reporter: 'I must say, sir, that you look in excellent health. To what do you owe your old age? Plenty of exercise? The right type of food?'

Grandfather: 'Not really. My old age is probably due more to my being born such a very long time ago.'

* * *

My grandfather likes to go to jumble sales. The other day he came home with a suit which he said would fit him like a glove: it had four trouser legs and one sleeve.

* * *

My grandfather had to travel up to town to see a Harley Street specialist. Unfortunately, this meant travelling during the rush hour from his small suburban station.

On boarding the train he found all the carriages full – except for one which had one seat occupied by a man's bulky briefcase.

'Is this seat taken?' he asked the man sitting next to the briefcase.

'I'm afraid so,' replied the man, without looking up from his newspaper. 'The owner has just nipped off the train to get a newspaper – I suggest you try another carriage.'

My grandfather thought this an unlikely tale, as the station did not have a newspaper kiosk. The newspaper-reading passenger probably wanted to reserve the seat for himself so that he could have more room.

This proved to be correct when the train resumed its journey. My grandfather snatched up the briefcase, threw it out of the window on to the platform, and sat down.

The passenger next to my grandfather was outraged. 'What the hell did you do that for?' he asked.

'I thought you said the briefcase belonged to a passenger who was buying a newspaper on the platform,' replied my grandfather. 'As the train obviously started off without him I thought he'd better have his briefcase.'

* * *

My grandfather recovered consciousness after a serious operation. He blinked, looked around the room, and croaked: 'Is it morning or night?'

'Neither,' replied the nurse. 'It's early afternoon.'

'Then why are the curtains closed?'

'Because the building directly opposite is on fire,' said the nurse, 'and we didn't want you to wake up and think the operation had failed.'

* * *

'Have you lived here in this little village all your life?' a tourist asked my grandfather.

'Not yet,' he replied.

* * *

My grandfather says he realized he was getting old when he found himself chasing girls but couldn't think why he was doing it.

* * *

My grandfather has been an actor for the past eighty years and has never won an award – until recently, when he was presented with a side of ham labelled: 'To Henry Truss, best supporting actor.'

* * *

Grandfather had lived all his life in a small shack in the woods. But now that he was eighty-six he was no longer able to cope with living in such dilapidated conditions.

I felt sorry for him, for I knew his health would suffer if he continued to live in the shack. So I invited him to move into a small seaside flat which I rented.

He was delighted. He spent most of the first day in the flat just walking around and marvelling at the miracles of modern life: a television, an electric cooker, a pop-up toaster.

Feeling that he was able to cope on his own, and knowing how much he cherished his independence, I left him in the flat and went back to my house, which is only a few miles away. I told grandfather that if he ever wanted anything, all he had to do was to pick up the phone and I would be there within fifteen minutes.

Early next morning, grandfather phoned.

'Is anything the matter?' I asked.

'No, not particularly,' he replied. 'But I'm a bit puzzled by this new-fangled washing-machine thing. When I put my shirt and underwear in it and pulled the chain, there was a sudden rush of water and they disappeared.'

* * *

My grandmother believes so strongly in reincarnation that she's made a will leaving all her money to herself.

* * *

My grandmother went into an insurance broker's office the other day and said she wanted to take out some life insurance.

'On your own life, madam?' asked the broker.

'Yes,' replied grandmother.

'How old are you?'

'One hundred and three,' she replied.

'Oh! I'm very sorry, but I can't help you. I doubt if any insurance company would be willing to write a policy on your life – it's such a high risk.'

'Rubbish!' snorted grandmother. 'You work on statistics, don't you?'

'Yes. Everything is based on actuarial statistical analysis.'

'Well then,' said grandmother, 'surely your own statistics will tell you that not many people aged a hundred and three die each year.'

* * *

Yesterday afternoon my grandmother was driving her car and busily knitting at the same time.

A police motorcyclist saw this, started his siren, and drew up alongside her car.

'Pull over,' he said.

'No,' replied grandmother, 'it's not a pullover – only a pair of socks.'

* * *

My grandmother is something of a gourmet and it was her life's ambition to visit a remote area of South America where, it was said, the people lived entirely by eating an especially exotic delicacy known as poiy.

For years she scrimped and saved to get enough money to make the journey to South America. At last she was able to make the trip and, after encountering many hazards on her journey through the forests and jungles of the region, she arrived at the remote village.

'I have come,' she said to the village leader, 'solely to sample your local delicacy – the poiy. I understand that you and your people eat nothing but poiy.'

'That is so,' replied the leader.

'No other peoples in the region eat this delicacy?'

'No. It is our diet because the village cook came to us from a distant land.'

'May I meet the cook?'

'Certainly. But first you must sample the poiy – would you like steak and kidney poiy, shepherd's poiy or potato poiy first? With apple or gooseberry poiy to follow?'

After the meal my grandmother met the cook – an Irishman from London who had come to the region many years before!

* * *

My grandmother recently painted her sundial with luminous paint. She said she wanted to be able to read the time at night.

* * *

One evening, in the middle of a thunderstorm, a young man knocked on my door.

'Would you like to assist the Old Folks' Home?' he asked.

'What are they doing walking about on a night like this?' I replied.

'You don't understand. They are at home already. What I want is a contribution to the home.'

So I gave him grandmother and shut the door.

* * *

The young mother had just arrived home from the hospital with her newly-born baby.

'Ah! How cute!' said grandmother, looking at the baby. 'And if I remember correctly,' she said, taking a closer look, 'it's a boy.'

* * *

The local television station sent out a film crew to interview the wonderful old grandmother who was celebrating her 105th birthday.

The interview went very well and the film crew were impressed with the wit and vitality of the old lady.

Just as they were packing up their equipment ready to leave, a young cameraman said to grandmother: 'Thanks very much for the tea and cakes. It's been a real pleasure meeting you. I hope I'm around to film you when you celebrate 110 years.'

Grandmother looked at him closely and said: 'I don't see why you shouldn't be around then – you look quite healthy.'

* * *

The important businessman was spending a weekend with his elderly grandmother.

'I'm expecting some urgent calls,' he said. 'So if anyone phones for me, can you take a message?'

'Yes, dear,' replied his grandmother. 'But where will you be?'

'I have to go to the shops to bring my wife back in the car – she's sure to be loaded with things she's bought.'

So the businessman set off for the shops and returned less than an hour later.

'Any calls for me?' he asked.

'No, dear. None for you. Only a strange woman kept calling.'

'A strange woman? What did she say?'

'Well, after she asked the phone number and checked that it was mine she said "Long distance from Cairo" and I replied "Yes, it is a long distance" and hung up.'

* * *

My grandmother was feeling a bit depressed so she went to her doctor and said: 'Doctor, I feel very fed up. How long do you think I'll live?'

The doctor paused, looked at her, and replied: 'Oh, you'll live to be ninety.'

'But I am ninety,' said grandmother.

'See,' said the doctor, 'didn't I tell you?'

* * *

Now that my grandmother's eyesight is failing she parks her car by ear.

* * *

Grandson: 'Aren't you pleased, gran, now that you've retired? You don't have to go to work any more and you can spend your days doing whatever you want.'

Grandmother: 'I'm not pleased at all. Time seems to hang very heavily on my hands.'

Grandson: 'Well, if you will insist on wearing that grandfather clock strapped to your wrist . . .'

* * *

The little old grandmother went up to the policeman and started poking at him with the end of her broom.

'Stop it! Stop it!' he cried. 'Why are you poking me with that broom?'

'Because,' said grandmother, 'I've led a boring, blameless life these past eighty-nine years so I thought it was about time I had a brush with the law.'

* * *

My grandmother is very short-sighted. When I showed her a photograph of my son on holiday at the seaside she pointed to the donkey in the picture and said: 'It's a good likeness of you, but what is that on your back?'

* * *

My grandmother's eyesight is not what it was. The other day she came rushing out of the house just as a fire engine raced along the street, its bells clanging.

As the fire engine disappeared around the corner she said: 'Huh! If you can't be bothered to wait for me, I can't be bothered to buy your terrible ice-cream!'

* * *

9

UNCLES

I have one uncle whom I've never met. If he reads this book, I'd like him to know I think about him, even though I don't know him.
This chapter is dedicated to Uncle Bernard.

* * *

Tom: 'My uncle reminds me of a film star.'
Samantha: 'Which one? Tony Curtis? Robert Redford?'
Tom: 'King Kong.'

* * *

My uncle made a real killing on the stock market this morning. He strangled his stockbroker.

* * *

Whenever my uncle goes to fancy dress parties he dresses as Napoleon so he can keep one hand on his wallet.

* * *

My uncle has a reputation for being a tough employer. You can't help but admire him – if you don't, he gives you the sack.

* * *

Last night my uncle went to a very posh function where he wore all his military medals.

The society hostess looked at him admiringly when he arrived: 'My,' she said, 'you *do* have a lot of medals. You must have been a real hero. What did you have to do to get all those?'

'Oh,' replied my uncle, 'all I had to do was pay £15.75 – I bought them at a local jumble sale.'

*　*　*

'What are you complaining about now?' I asked my uncle.

'It's that brother of yours.'

'What about him?'

'Well, he's the *dearest* relative I've ever had. He's just got married for the second time – so that's two wedding presents and a wreath he's cost me in the past six years.'

*　*　*

The telephone rang. I picked it up and my mother's voice said: 'It's good news at last! Your sister gave birth half an hour ago – but I haven't been able to find out from the hospital yet whether it's a boy or a girl, so I can't tell you if you're now an uncle or an aunt.'

*　*　*

My uncle is a very successful businessman and so I thought I should ask his advice before setting up in business myself.

'What business do you think I ought to go in for to make the most money?' I asked. 'And is there any special way I ought to run the business to be more successful than others?'

'My boy,' he replied, 'there are thousands of different ways to make a fortune in business, but there's only one honest way.'

'What way is that?' I enquired eagerly.

'How would I know?'

*　*　*

My uncle Cuthbert is the most miserly man in the world.

A friend of mine once called on him hoping for a large donation to the friend's favourite charity.

'Listen, young man,' said my uncle. 'I'm sure you think your charity is worthwhile . . . '

'Oh, it is!'

'Don't interrupt!' snapped my uncle. 'You may think I've got a lot of money because I own a number of very profitable companies. But bear in mind that I have an extremely large family. Both my sons have been undergoing expensive hospital treatment for the past fifteen years; my daughter has been recently widowed, leaving her with no source of income and seven children to support; my own parents live on an island which has just been devastated by an earthquake so now they are homeless; and my wife has been kidnapped by criminals who are demanding £2 million or they will chop off her arms and legs and then kill her.'

'Oh,' said my friend. 'I didn't know your family were costing you so much money.'

'They're not,' replied my uncle. 'I don't pay my sons' medical expenses, I'm not supporting my daughter, my parents can stay homeless for all I care, and my wife is welcome to be chopped up by her kidnappers. So you can see – if I'm not prepared to help my own family financially, how can you expect me to help your charity and people I don't even know?'

* * *

My uncle Edgar is a rather eccentric inventor. His latest creation is music printed on sheets of polythene for people who want to play underwater.

* * *

One of my uncles, who is Irish, went to his dentist and asked him to put *in* a wisdom tooth.

* * *

When my uncle Egbert kept having restless nights he went to see his doctor.
Egbert: 'What can I do to get a good night's sleep? It seems to take ages to fall asleep and even then I really only doze and keep waking up.'
Doctor: 'Have you tried counting sheep?'
Egbert: 'But I can't do that!'
Doctor: 'Why not?'
Egbert: 'Because I'm a vegetarian.'

* * *

When my uncle was offered a very cheap pocket calculator he refused to buy it because he said he already knew how many pockets he had.

* * *

One of my uncles is a statistician working for the Government. He's just finished a fifteen-year study on marriage trends in Britain and has come up with the conclusion that fifty per cent of all the people who get married are female. He'll probably spend another fifteen years trying to find out what the other fifty per cent are.

* * *

During the last war my uncle managed to put over 1000 people out of action in just one week – that was the week he was the cook for the camp.

* * *

My uncle is so mean he's even got padlocks attached to his dustbins.

* * *

My uncle went to the doctor saying he'd got terrible stomach problems.

After examining him for about ten minutes, the doctor said: 'I can't find anything seriously wrong with you. Of course, you're grossly overweight, but internally there seems to be nothing wrong. What exactly is this terrible stomach problem you complain about?'

My uncle replied: 'I can't do up my shirt buttons over it.'

* * *

Adrian: 'Why is your uncle behaving like that?'
Nigel: 'Behaving like what?'
Adrian: 'Well, just look at him! He's jogging all over the garden making a noise like a sports car and whenever he sees a rose bush he makes a sound like a car horn.'
Nigel: 'Oh, he's just being his usual self. He thinks he's a sports car.'
Adrian: 'But can't you stop him?'
Nigel: 'Why should I? He pays me £50 a week just to wax and polish him.'

* * *

One of my uncles is a member of the nobility – an hereditary peer, no less! The other day he had a terrible dream about making a speech in the House of Lords during which everyone dozed off. When my uncle woke up he found he really was in the House of Lords making the speech . . .

* * *

The Russian version of the above joke concerns an important Party official (another of my uncles) who fell asleep during a political rally in Russia during 1980 and kept shouting in his sleep: 'Down with Gromyko! Down with Gromyko!'

His colleagues urgently nudged him awake. 'What were you dreaming,' they asked, 'to make you shout such terrible things?'

'Well,' replied my Russian uncle, 'that was what everyone was chanting in the dream – I was at a political rally in 1990.'

* * *

One of my uncles, who lives in Ireland, went on a mystery coach tour. All the people on the coach put £5 into a hat – the winner of the money would be the person who correctly guessed where the coach would end up. Everyone was most surprised (even the winner) when the coach driver won the prize.

* * *

The only place my miserable old uncle will find health, wealth and happiness is in a dictionary.

* * *

My uncle was complaining about his health.

'What's wrong now?' I asked.

'I have to go into hospital again,' he replied.

'What is there to be upset about? You've been in hospital for minor ailments before.'

'Minor ailments?' he retorted. 'First I had stomach pains and I went in and they took out my appendix; then my throat was terribly sore so I went in and they took out my tonsils; and now I have terrible headaches I've got to go in . . . '

* * *

My uncle was asked if he would like to join the ATA – the Anti-Tipping Association. Being as mean as he is, my uncle naturally agreed with the Association's main aim of outlawing tipping. But when he found out that the subscription was fifty pence per year he said: 'I would save more in a year by paying my usual tips instead.'

* * *

My uncle is the most honest politician I know. When he's bought he stays bought.

* * *

Throughout his life my very rich uncle was a cantankerous, obstinate, and rather horrible creature, so when he was taken sick his wife asked the doctor: 'Is there no hope?'

'That depends on what you are hoping for.'

* * *

My uncle met his match in meanness with his boss.

'Can I have a day off work?' asked my uncle.

'What for?' demanded his boss.

'It's my Golden Wedding anniversary and . . .'

'What? Have a day off for that and set a precedent? You'll then be wanting a day off every fifty years . . .'

* * *

My uncle is a famous politician, but if he had to restrict himself to talking about things he understood, the silence would be total.

* * *

When my uncle was in the army and had to go into battle for the first time he was frightened stiff when the enemy started firing and lobbing hand grenades at him. He jumped out of his trench and ran away as fast as his legs would carry him.

After running for some time he collapsed in a nervous heap at the feet of another soldier.

'Get up!' commanded the soldier. 'Get up, private, get up!'

My uncle looked up and saw it was a colonel. 'Goodness!' gasped my uncle. 'I didn't know I'd run that far.'

* * *

10

AUNTS

I tried to write a poem about aunts, but when I read the result I decided I'd better stick to being a comedian. Anyway, this chapter is dedicated to Auntie Peggy.

* * *

My aunt's doctor put her on a diet of garlic and beans. She didn't lose any weight – but she did lose all her friends.

* * *

My Aunt Gladys is always attending charity balls – she loves to dress up in her expensive furs and mingle with the nobility.

One evening as she was waiting for a taxi in Park Lane to take her home, a tramp came up to her and said: 'I haven't eaten for three days.'

'Well, you should force yourself,' replied my aunt. 'In your condition you shouldn't go on such silly diets.'

'But madam, I have no money. Can't you spare a pound so I can eat?'

'Goodness!' exclaimed Aunt Gladys. 'Here I am, absolutely worn out with dancing all night at a charity ball to help people like you and now you hang about asking for cash as well!'

* * *

One of my aunts is so nosy that she recently went to a Harley Street specialist to see if she could be fitted with an overhearing aid.

* * *

My aunt is a very successful dress designer – but success not only went to her head, it also went to her mouth.

* * *

My aunt was in a posh restaurant the other day when the waiter brought her soup with his finger in the bowl.

When she pointed this out to him, suggesting that he should carry the bowl properly, the waiter calmly replied: 'It's all right, madam. The soup's not hot – I won't burn my finger.'

* * *

My aunt was playing the piano in her flat one afternoon when the doorbell rang.

She opened the door and a man said: 'Good afternoon. I've come to tune your piano.'

'But I didn't ask you to call,' protested my aunt. 'I don't want my piano tuned.'

'No, lady,' said the piano tuner, 'you may not, but the people in the flat above you certainly do!'

* * *

When my aunt retired she decided to take up writing novels as a hobby – hoping one day that she would be successful. As her real name was Gladys Snitterby-Crouch-Gargleblurber she decided she ought to write under a pen-name – so she recently sent off her first manuscript to a publisher using the pen-name 'Fountain Italic-Nib'.

* * *

My aunt is something of a hypochondriac (in fact, she's so huge she looks more like a hippo-chondriac). Anyway, she recently went to her doctor and complained that she sometimes sneezed two or three times a day.

'It's probably just a bit of dust getting up your nose,' said the doctor. 'It's nothing to worry about.'

'But you must *do* something!' she insisted. 'Give me a full check-up, write a prescription for some pills . . . '

'Now, now,' soothed the doctor. 'You mustn't make much achoo about nothing.'

* * *

My aunt has such an enormous mouth that it takes her half an hour just to put her lipstick on.

* * *

My aunt, who weighs 35 stones, recently got engaged to a man who weighs 63 stones. They are planning to have a big wedding.

* * *

My aunt, who believes in corporal punishment (she also believes in sergeant, major, colonel and all other ranks punishment), thinks that the world treats criminals too kindly.

'Why,' she said to me the other day, 'I hear that prison life is so wonderful that bars have to be fitted to the cells to stop people breaking in.'

* * *

My aunt was the hostess at a very posh dinner at her home in Chelsea. It seemed to be going quite well, except that one of her oldest friends, the somewhat short-sighted Henrietta Blogsby-Pugh, was tending to ignore the man sitting on her right and paying all her attention to the elderly gentleman sitting on her left.

My aunt scribbled a note and gave it to her butler to pass on to Henrietta. Unfortunately, Henrietta had left her spectacles at home and so she asked the man on her right if he would kindly read the note for her.

The man looked at the note and read: 'Henrietta, darling, I *do* hope you won't mind me writing this – but please can you talk to the man on your right. I know he's the most dreadful bore, but . . . '

* * *

'Help! Help!' screamed my aunt from her study.

I rushed to her and asked: 'What's the matter?'

'I've swallowed my pencil!' she wailed. 'What am I going to do?'

'Well,' I replied, 'if the deadline for your new book is that pressing, can't you write with a pen?'

* * *

My aunt is an artist and I asked her if she liked painting people in the nude. She replied: 'At my age I need to keep my clothes on – I feel the cold terribly.'

* * *

My aunt Clarissa recently moved into a spacious new house in the country.

As she was proudly showing one of her friends around, the friend said: 'It's a really beautiful home. But I do feel you should have a chandelier in the lounge.'

'But I can't play one,' replied my aunt.

* * *

My aunt went on trial last week accused of murdering her husband – but the jury acquitted her because they felt sorry for her as she was a widow.

* * *

My aunt was on a train to Scunthorpe when a man came into her first-class carriage and sat opposite her.

After some minutes, the man and my aunt struck up a conversation.

'Are you going to Scunthorpe to attend that boring political conference?' my aunt enquired.

'Yes,' replied the man.

'I can't see why anyone goes to it – it's so terribly dull and dreary and the speakers drone on and on. The only reason I'm going is because my nephew is one of the party officials.'

'And the only reason I'm going,' commented the man, 'is because I'm one of the principal speakers.'

* * *

Nigel: 'Doctor, my aunt keeps me awake at night.'
Doctor: 'How?'
Nigel: 'She thinks she's a chicken and spends the whole night making loud clucking noises.'
Doctor: 'So you want me to stop her thinking she's a chicken?'
Nigel: 'No. Just stop her clucking so loud – the eggs she lays are very nice for breakfast.'

* * *

My aunt is so conceited that her only interest in life is herself.

* * *

I took my aunt to an exhibition of modern art the other day. As we walked around the gallery she criticized all the paintings and sculptures saying, 'Rubbish! Absolute rubbish!' and 'I can't imagine what anyone sees in all this modern art stuff. Even children could do better!'

Then she came to something which stopped her dead in her tracks. 'Appalling!' she snapped. 'Really appalling! It looks like nothing on earth – and yet I suppose it's meant to look like a hideously ugly old crone.'

'Perhaps,' I said, 'but you're looking at a mirror.'

*   *   *

11

COUSINS

My mother comes from a large family. She's got four sisters and five brothers. I've got at least forty cousins to date. So with a little stretch of the imagination this is what could happen: forty first cousins have between them sixty sons and daughters. Sixty second cousins produce a new generation of eighty children. That makes 180 members of the Yarwood clan. If I go any further, the whole world will be peopled with Yarwoods! This chapter is dedicated to Cousins Eamonn and Christopher.

* * *

My cousin went to the doctor this morning and said: 'Doctor, can you help me? People keep thinking I'm a cricket ball.'

'How's that?' asked the doctor.

'Huh!' muttered my cousin. 'You think so, too!'

* * *

My cousin Lionel is a terrible old drunkard. The other weekend he came to visit me and was bitterly complaining about his train journey.

'What happened?' I asked.

'I lost all my luggage,' he moaned. 'The cork came out . . .'

* * *

My cousin was run over by a steamroller this morning – now he's in hospital in wards ten, eleven, twelve, thirteen and fourteen.

* * *

My cousin and I went to a small Italian restaurant last night. After waiting for a considerable time before a waiter even bothered to take our orders, we had even longer to wait before the first course arrived.

'Will the spaghetti be long?' asked my cousin, while we waited for the main course.

'Not really,' replied the waiter. 'Just the usual length – about 12 to 18 inches.'

* * *

My cousin Alfred is a psychiatrist, so I was not surprised when I discovered that his daughter never played with the doll I bought her for Christmas: all she did with it was to lay it on the sofa and ask it questions.

* * *

When my cousin went to hospital the other day to have an operation, the surgeon told him that they had run out of anaesthetic so he was forced to watch a Party Political Broadcast in order to be put into a deep enough sleep.

* * *

My cousin Robert wants to be a famous writer. Indeed, he's just written something which he knows will be accepted by a top national magazine: a cheque for a five-year subscription.

* * *

My cousin George is 9 feet 6 inches tall. When he went for a job as a lifeguard at a busy seaside resort he admitted that he could not swim, but said: 'You should see me when I paddle!'

* * *

When my cousin Louisa started work as a secretary and was told by her boss to file some letters, she said: 'But filing them will take ages – couldn't I trim them down with scissors instead?'

* * *

My cousin Dora is rather a know-it-all. I asked her if she'd ever ridden a horse, and she said: 'Of course.' So I asked her to come riding with me one weekend.

Just as we were saddling up, I noticed that she was putting the saddle on the wrong way round. 'The saddle should be facing the other way,' I said.

'Huh!' she snapped. 'How do *you* know which direction I shall be riding in?'

* * *

'I'm fed up with you walking into my bedroom without knocking!' said my cousin Wilhelmina to her manservant.

'Sorry, madam,' he replied. 'But I do always look through the keyhole first before entering, so you can be assured that I'd never come in when you are undressed.'

* * *

My cousin Tom had a difficult time stuffing the Christmas turkey – his wife said that if he'd stuffed it much more he would have killed it.

* * *

My cousin Pauline wears so much deodorant, hair spray, nail varnish, and anti-perspirant that her boyfriend says he feels he's going out with a chemical company.

* * *

My cousin and I went to a disco recently which was so crowded that my cousin fainted but couldn't fall down for half an hour.

* * *

One of my cousins is a kung-fu expert. The other day he hit a mosquito on his side and broke three ribs.

* * *

Adrian had a very bad stutter and asked me to help.

We struggled with this problem for months until finally he could say things like 'round the rugged rocks the ragged rascals ran' and 'shut up the shutters and sit in the shop'.

But after all my hard work and effort Adrian had the nerve to say: 'It's all v-v-very w-w-well b-b-being able to say "round the rugged rocks the ragged rascals ran", b-b-but it's v-v-very d-d-difficult to w-w-work into a c-c-conversation.'

* * *

One of my cousins is such a lazy farmer that he's spent years trying to cross a parrot with a hen: he's trying to breed a creature that comes and tells him when it's laid an egg.

* * *

The same cousin I just mentioned is also a bit crazy. He once put seven ducks in a cardboard box because he wanted a box of quackers.

* * *

Fiona is the most conceited cousin I know. One day I overheard a conversation between her and her boyfriend.
Fiona: 'Do you think I'm a bit conceited?'
Boyfriend: 'No, of course not. Why do you ask that?'
Fiona: 'Because girls as pretty, witty, intelligent and generally as adorable as me are usually a bit conceited about it.'

* * *

Petronella, another cousin of mine, says she's only thirty-nine. As she's been saying it for the past fifteen years and always sticks to the same story, I suppose it must be true.

* * *

'Come on!' I called to my cousin, Louisa, who was in her bedroom. 'If you don't hurry we'll be late for the concert.'

'All right! All right!' called Louisa. 'Stop hounding me! Didn't I tell you only half an hour ago that I'd be ready in a minute?'

* * *

My cousin Cecil is a statistician. He's the sort of fellow who will confidently tell you that if your head is in the refrigerator and your feet in the oven, overall you'll be quite comfortable.

* * *

My cousin Jane was asked by a friend of mine if she would marry him. 'I'm young, reasonably handsome, and my father is worth millions,' he said. 'And I'm my father's only heir so when he dies I shall inherit everything.'

'How old is your father?' Jane asked.

'Ninety-six,' replied my friend.

One month later, Jane married my friend's father!

* * *

My cousin's boss roared at him: 'Alan! You're late again. Don't you know what time we start work here?'

'No, sir,' replied my cousin. 'Everyone always seems to be hard at work when I arrive.'

* * *

My cousin married a girl who was one of triplets.

'How do you tell them apart?' I asked.

'Easy!' replied my cousin. 'The other two have got beards and moustaches.'

* * *

My cousin Fatima is so ugly that when she goes to the beach in her bikini all the men turn their heads – away! She's so fat that if she ever became a stripper she'd have to wear a G-rope.

* * *

My cousin Albert is a politician: he falls for everything and stands for nothing.

* * *

When my lawyer cousin was seriously ill I visited him in hospital, and found him eagerly reading the Bible.

'I didn't know you were religious,' I said.

'I'm not,' he replied. 'I'm just looking for loopholes.'

* * *

My cousin Algernon was flying along in his small aeroplane when suddenly the engines stopped.

He radioed the airport control tower and was asked: 'What is your exact height and position?'

'Well,' he replied, 'I don't know exactly. But I think I'm

about 5 feet $8\frac{1}{2}$ inches tall, and I'm sitting at the aircraft controls.'

* * *

One of my cousins, Dick Shunnery, works in a library, so I asked him if he could recommend some books which were a good read. He gave me the following:
Annoying Bed Companions by Constance Norah
No Food by M. T. Freezer
Baby-sitting Hints by Justin Casey-Howells
Lion-taming For All by Claude Bottom
How To Make A Horse Jump by Jim Karna
Easy Ways Of Getting Money by Robin Banks
Hypochondriac Symptoms by Mona Lott
How To Succeed In Everything by Percy Vere
The Long Unhappy Walk by Miss D. Buss
What Do I Do With A Naughty Boy? by Enid Spankin
Rice-growing In Ireland by Paddy Fields
Simple Carpet Fitting by Walter Wall

* * *

One of my cousins says that middle age is when your narrow waist and broad mind change places.

* * *

My cousin Clive came home from work totally exhausted yesterday evening.

'What happened?' I asked. 'You look totally worn out.'

'I know,' he replied. 'The company computer broke down and everyone actually had to think!'

* * *

A cheeky young man once said to my pretty cousin: 'If you give me a kiss, I'll show you the world.'

She gave him a kiss and he gave her an atlas.

* * *

My cousin Arnold, a commercial traveller, went into a pub the other day and got chatting to the locals. Arnold explained that although it was his first visit to the region he hoped he would often be able to visit the pub as its surroundings were so beautiful.

The locals seemed to accept Arnold and after many more drinks the talk turned to politics.

'I can't stand Mrs Thatcher,' said one of the locals.

'I don't like Jim Callaghan,' confessed Arnold. 'His face looks like a sheep's head.'

Ten minutes later, Arnold came to in the pub car park. He'd been badly beaten up.

'What did you do that for?' he asked. 'I didn't know anyone felt that strongly about Jim Callaghan. Is this Labour territory or something?'

'No,' replied the locals, 'sheep territory.'

* * *

12

DISTANT RELATIVES

You never know, if your name is Yarwood you might be a distant relative of mine, because Yarwood is my real name. I suppose people use a stage name in showbusiness to have a bit more privacy, but using your real name can have its advantages, like when it comes to cashing cheques!

It also means I get news from the Yarwoods of the world. I had a letter once from a man in Australia who thought he might be a long-lost relative, and I took it as a compliment that he wanted to be part of my family. There could be risks involved though, which is why I joke about it, because you don't know who'll turn up on your doorstep next!

* * *

One of my relatives is so distant that he thinks Ellesmere Port is a new type of drink from Portugal.

* * *

Mr and Mrs Gringleworthy were very excited. They had just received a telegram to say that a very distant relative would be arriving in England from Outer Mongolia and that she would be delighted to see them at the airport.

The Gringleworthys had known about their relative in Mongolia for some years, but their correspondence had been limited to little more than the exchange of cards at Christmas.

As they waited at the airport, Mrs Gringleworthy asked her husband: 'Do you think she'll be able to speak much English? Her cards were always very brief and I'd hate not to be able to communicate with her properly.'

Before she could say any more (not that she wanted to say 'any more') the relative arrived: a rather portly, middle-aged lady dressed in ill-fitting clothes and carrying a cheap suitcase.

'Welcome to England,' said Mr Gringleworthy.

'Scccch . . . weee . . . hello. I pleased to sccch . . . wee . . . meet you,' replied the relative.

'Let me take your suitcase,' offered Mr Gringleworthy.

'Scccch . . . weee . . . thank you. I very sch . . . weee . . . grateful. I receive your nice sch . . . weee . . . card. Bring you small scccch . . . weeee . . . present from home sccchh . . . weeee . . . country.'

'Your English is very good,' said Mrs Gringleworthy. 'I was a bit worried we might not be able to communicate. Where did you learn English?'

'At home by sccch . . . weee . . . listening to the scccch . . . weeee . . . English from overseas sccch . . . weeee . . . service of BBC.'

* * *

One of my distant relatives comes from a long line of boxers. As for myself, I think I come from a long line of golden retrievers.

* * *

Another of my relatives was sunbathing with a fellow surgeon at a south coast resort when a beautiful girl walked past.

'What fantastic legs!' sighed my relative.

'Actually,' replied his friend, 'I'm a chest man, myself.'

* * *

This reminds me of another very old distant relative who was chatting up a pretty young girl when she suddenly asked him: 'What sort of medical man are you?'

'I'm a naval surgeon,' he replied.

'Goodness!' exclaimed the girl. 'I knew people specialized in ears, noses, throats, chests, hearts and ears – but to specialize just in belly buttons . . . '

* * *

Which reminds me: another of my distant relatives is a famous American film star. She's had so many face-lifts that the dimple in her chin is really her navel.

* * *

One of my relatives invited me to a party in Scotland last weekend. I went to the party and found the drinks flowed like glue.

* * *

Every family has its black sheep. Fortunately, my safe-breaking relative always uses his toes when fiddling with combination locks. It's driving the police fingerprint experts wild!

* * *

Another relative of mine invited me to her palatial mansion in the country for the weekend.

'I must warn you,' said my relative, 'that my new maid hasn't been broken-in properly yet. Staff are so difficult to find these days that one just has to accept what one can get and hope that one can train them suitably.'

I found out what she meant when the maid served the salad. She entered the room completely naked. Everyone was stunned – especially as the maid was forty-three and ugly.

'Henrietta!' shrieked my relative. 'Go and put some clothes on this instant! Whatever do you think you're doing?'

'But,' protested the maid, 'you specifically told me to make sure the salad was served without dressing.'

* * *

One of my relatives is partly of Welsh extraction: he once went to a dentist in Cardiff who took out one of his wisdom teeth.

* * *

One of my distant relatives is a cannibal. He used to suffer from terrible indigestion because he ate people who disagreed with him.

* * *

The same relative used to have great fun with his friends at parties – they played swallow my leader.

* * *

But he was very useful when he came to England. I let him put the bite on my moneylender.

* * *

His sister was a vegetarian cannibal – she would only eat Swedes.

* * *

The other day my cannibal relative complained to me: 'You know, that missionary I ate this morning keeps making me feel sick.'

I told him, 'The reason for that is obvious: you can't keep a good man down.'

* * *

The cannibal's sister, when she reached the age of eighteen, started to look in earnest for an edible bachelor.

* * *

When my cannibal relative started getting too fat his doctor put him on a diet. Now he is only allowed to eat midgets.

* * *

My cannibal relative's greatest ambition is to become a detective-inspector – then he can grill all his suspects.

* * *

When I went to my cannibal relative's wedding, all the guests enjoyed toasting his mother-in-law.

* * *

My cannibal relative likes his soup with plenty of body in it.

* * *

My cannibal relative complained about the other guests in the London hotel where he was staying.

'What's wrong with them?' I asked.

'As soon as I get in my room they start banging on the walls, banging on the door, and even banging on the ceiling – they bang so loud I can hardly hear myself playing my war drums.'

* * *

My cannibal relative went to a Chinese take-away last night and took home two Chinese. Trouble was, fifteen minutes after eating them he felt hungry again.

* * *

Some of my more distant relatives are dead, and every year at Christmas they put on their own production of *Cinderella*. I suppose you could call it a phantomime.

* * *

Several of my ghost relatives are short-sighted and have to wear spooktacles.

* * *

Then there's my Irish distant relative who believed in reincarnation. He did, actually, come back to earth as an Irish tadpole – which later turned into a butterfly.

* * *

The trouble with visiting distant relatives is that they can be so distant. On the way to visit a relative in Australia the ship tossed and turned so much that I kept being sick.

When the steward came to my cabin with my breakfast I told him to throw it overboard and save me the trouble!

* * *

Another relative of mine is a historian in Russia – he writes loose-leaf history books.

* * *

And yet another relative makes acoustical devices for deaf fishermen – he calls them herring aids.

* * *

One of my relatives used to be dreadfully nagged at by his house-proud wife. He had to take off his shoes before he was allowed into the house; he couldn't smoke for fear the cigarette ash might fall on to the carpet; he had to sit upright in his chair to watch television in case he crumpled the fabric of the chair covering; and he had to hang his clothes up neatly every evening before going to bed.

My relative had his revenge, however, when he died. In his will he stipulated that he was to be cremated and his ashes were to be scattered over the lounge carpet.

* * *

I asked a distant relative of mine if any famous men had been born in his home town. He replied: 'No. The women in my town only give birth to babies.'

* * *

A relative of mine whom I had not seen for many years recently arrived in England and I took him to lunch.

Near the end of the meal – which my relative insisted was to be a treat on him – my relative asked the waiter: 'Please can I have some *petit fours*?'

The waiter looked blankly at him, scratched his head, then exclaimed: 'Ah! Sir has been away from England for many years?'

'Yes,' agreed my relative.

'Then he would not know that with inflation there are no longer *petit fours* – they are now called *petit eights*.'

* * *

One of my relatives is a midget. He recently went on holiday to a nudist camp – but was thrown out because he couldn't keep his nose out of other people's private affairs.

* * *

A distant relative of mine lives in a very remote region of the world where most people travel by mule.

He recently visited England for the first time and had to make a journey across London by tube.

As he was sitting in the underground railway carriage he lit a cigarette.

'Hey!' said one of the other passengers. 'Can't you see the signs? This is a *No Smoking* carriage.'

'I'm sorry, I'm a stranger. But do you really expect me to follow all your signs? There's one up there,' said my relative, pointing to an advertisement, 'which says "Wear A Better Bra Today".'

* * *

I was on my way to meet a relative in Sydney, Australia, and as I drove along the strange Australian roads I thought I might be getting lost. So I stopped the car and asked a little old lady who was walking by the side of the road, 'Do you know the way to Sydney?'

'Yes,' she replied, and continued walking.

* * *

One of my relatives, who is Polish, went to his optician the other day.

'Can you read the first three lines on this card?' asked the optician, pointing to a card on which the first three lines were set out like this:

C

ZES

TOCHOWA

'I can not only read it,' replied my relative, 'but I've been there – it's not far from Czechoslovakia.'

* * *

Henrietta Gloomer is a famous Hollywood actress – who also

happens to be a distant relative of mine.

I only met her once, and that was during a murder trial when she was one of the witnesses for the prosecution.

'Please identify yourself,' said the lawyer when Henrietta took the witness stand.

'I'm Henrietta Gloomer – the world's leading and best actress.'

At the end of the day's hearing I said to Henrietta: 'I thought you were always very modest about your acting ability, unlike some other stars. So why did you describe yourself in court as the world's leading and best actress?'

'I had to,' replied Henrietta, 'as I was under oath to tell only the truth.'

* * *

A distant relative of mine wanted to meet me in England. He couldn't afford the boat or air fare, so he decided to swim across the water to Cornwall.

I was late in meeting him on the beach after his exhausting journey.

'Huh!' he said. 'I swim all this way just to meet you, and you can't even arrive on time.'

'I'm sorry,' I replied, 'but I thought the Channel crossing this time of year would be rather rough and that you would be late.'

'Channel?' he said. 'Channel? I thought you knew I lived in Florida – I've just swum the Atlantic!'

* * *

A young relative of mine recently sent off for a body-building course.

The relative followed all the instructions and now has a very muscular chest, arms, legs and back – and looks a real 'He man.' But why Gladys should want to look like that, I don't know!

* * *

One of my Scottish relatives had to get married recently. He won a honeymoon for two in Paris in a free newspaper competition and he didn't want to waste the prize.

* * *

One of my distant relatives, whom I prefer to keep quiet about, is a Russian spy.

Last weekend he had to visit Cardiff in order to make contact with a local agent.

On arriving at the agent's address, he was horrified to discover that it was a block of flats – and fifteen people had the same name as the agent, Evans.

Taking a chance, my relative knocked on the door of one of the flats, and when the door opened he said: 'Evans?'

'Yes,' replied the man.

'The swallows are migrating early this year,' said my relative, giving the password.

'Oh,' said Mr Evans. 'I'm only Evans-the-milk, the local milkman. You want Evans-the-spy – he's got the flat two floors up.'

* * *

13

PETS

I used to have a dog called Shep who lived until he was fourteen. I was very upset when he died. We don't have any pets now because we're never at home long enough to look after them, but everyone tells me their pets are very amusing. So here are a few pet jokes I hope you'll find amusing, too.

* * *

The other day I found my German neighbour laying his pet snake across the windscreen of his car.

'What are you doing?' I asked. 'If you drive your car with the snake like that, he'll fall off.'

'Don't worry,' replied the neighbour, 'it's a vindscreen viper.'

* * *

Last Sunday I had lunch with a friend at his home and throughout the meal his pet dog kept looking at me and wagging his tail.

'He seems a really friendly dog,' I said.

'Yes,' said my friend.

'Is he like this with everyone?' I asked.

'Oh, no! It's just that you're eating off his plate.'

* * *

A person I know has a pet hen. He gives it boiling water to drink every night in the hope that it'll lay hard-boiled eggs.

* * *

The other day two small kids knocked on my door saying they were collecting for the local zoo. They needed some help in making a better pool for the pet penguins so I gave them a bucket of water.

* * *

Last night my wife interrupted my dozing by our nice log fire and said: 'Put the cat out.'

'What for?' I asked, looking at my watch. 'It's early yet.'

'Because,' replied my wife, 'a log has just fallen out of the grate and the cat's on fire.'

* * *

James: 'I'm taking my pet tortoise to a psychiatrist.'
Lionel: 'Why?'
James: 'Because he seems very shy – I'm hoping the psychiatrist can help me to bring him out of his shell.'

* * *

Adrian: 'My pet cat can have something no other animal can.'
Clive: 'Oh, and what's that?'
Adrian: 'Kittens.'

* * *

Paul's dog was once faced with four trees – he didn't have a leg to stand on.

* * *

I took my pet dog to the vet this morning because he bit my mother-in-law. I have to collect him this afternoon after his teeth have been sharpened.

* * *

Henry Molesworthy kept a pet aardvark which looked a bit depressed. No matter how much he tried to cheer up the aardvark, the creature still had a mournful expression, so Henry decided to take his pet to the vet.

The vet – who was Austrian – gave the aardvark a complete examination, and then said: 'Ah! Vat he needs iss complete rest. He hass been varking too aard.'

* * *

Claude: 'I've just lost my pet baboon.'
Prunella: 'Why don't you put an advertisement in the local paper?'
Claude: 'That wouldn't do any good – he can't read.'

* * *

A man I know once crossed a police dog with a Scots terrier. It's a really incredible dog – it's so strong it can toss a caber and then run and fetch it.

* * *

My pet lemming was suffering from the effects of a hot summer's day and looked very thirsty – so I went and bought him some lemming-aid.

* * *

My Uncle Edgar was shopping in the High Street the other day when he found a large orang-utan walking along in the gutter.

Being very fond of animals, Uncle Edgar rescued the creature and took it to a policeman who was directing traffic in the middle of the road.

'What's that?' asked the policeman.

'It's an orang-utan,' replied my uncle. 'I found it in the gutter. What should I do with it?'

'Well,' said the policeman, 'I've got to stay here directing the traffic, but if I were you I'd take the creature to the zoo.'

The next day my uncle walked down the High Street with the orang-utan on a lead behind him.

'Hey!' called the policeman from the middle of the road. 'I thought you were going to take that animal to the zoo?'

'I did,' replied Uncle Edgar. 'I think he quite enjoyed it, so now I'm taking him to the cinema – and perhaps tomorrow we'll go to the theatre.'

* * *

Our puppy is called Carpenter – because he's always doing little jobs around the house.

* * *

I called on a friend the other day and as I rang his doorbell, I could hear his pet dog barking and growling.

'Is your dog safe?' I called through the letterbox, somewhat afraid that when the door was open the dog might tear me to pieces.

'Of course,' my friend called back. 'You've heard of the saying "A barking dog never bites?" '

'Yes,' I replied. 'I've heard of it, you've heard of it – but has the dog heard of it?'

* * *

A business colleague of mine keeps an aquarium full of fish on his office desk. When I asked him if he was fond of goldfish, he replied: 'Very. When things get hectic I can just relax and look at them opening and closing their mouths – without asking for a pay rise.'

* * *

During the recent sheep dog trials, seven were found guilty and ten were acquitted.

* * *

Ron: 'Why does your pet aardvark have that stupid grin on its face?'
Henry: 'Because he really is stupid.'

* * *

An old lady died and all her personal effects were to be auctioned – including her pet parrot.

As the bidding for the parrot progressed, it became clear that it was a contest between two rivals – and eventually the parrot went for a record £250.

'I've paid a huge sum of money for this parrot,' said the successful bidder to the auctioneer. 'In fact, I paid ten times what I had intended to offer – but I got carried away in the excitement of the auction room. But having paid all that money, I do hope he can talk.'

'Of course he can,' replied the auctioneer. 'Who do you think was bidding against you?'

* * *

A man who kept five pet alligators often used to feed them dead human bodies, since he had a special arrangement with a crooked undertaker.

One day the alligators were discussing which type of human they liked best.

'I like actors,' said one of the alligators.

)h, I can't eat them,' replied another. 'I'm Jewish and I'm ııuı allowed to touch ham.'

But all the alligators eventually agreed that the tastiest human was a politician – once the wind inside them had escaped they were soft, fleshy and had no backbone.

* * *

Gladys: 'Husband, dear, I think our pet dog is getting old.'
Fred: 'Why do you say that, dear?'
Gladys: 'He seems to be going a bit deaf.'
Fred: 'Nonsense! Here. I'll show you.'

Fred turns to the dog and says: 'Rover, sit!'

A few seconds later, Fred turns to Gladys and says: 'You were right. I'll go and get a shovel and clear it up.'

* * *

A man was shipwrecked on a desert island – with only his pet parrot to keep him company.

As he looked around the island, the man said to his parrot: 'I suppose it could be worse.'

And the parrot said: 'Of course it could! You could have bought a return ticket!'

* * *

Jim used to keep pet snakes. One day one of the snakes turned to his friend and said: 'Do you know if we're poisonous?'

'Why do you want to know?' asked the other snake.

'Because I've just bitten my bottom lip.'

* * *

For years, Stuart had been training his pet tortoise to sing while his pet aardvark played the piano with its nose.

At last he felt they were ready to perform in public and so took them to a theatrical agent.

The agent was impressed, but said: 'It's so remarkable there must be a trick in it somewhere. Are you a ventriloquist for the tortoise? I don't mind what the trick is – the act will stand up before the public. But you must tell me what it is.'

So Stuart reluctantly explained that not only did the aardvark play piano, but it was also the ventriloquist for the tortoise.

* * *

My dog is very fond of children – but I think he prefers biscuits.

* * *

A friend of mine has a pet camel with three humps. He calls it Humphrey.

* * *

A friend of mine has a pet elephant, but he got so fed up with people commenting on the creature when he took it for walks in the park that now whenever they go out together he makes the elephant wear a disguise: dark glasses and a moustache.

* * *

Charles had a terrible stammer and bought a pet parrot in the hope that the parrot would teach him to talk properly.

One day the parrot looked a bit thin so Charles went to a pet shop and asked: 'H-h-have y-y-ou any b-b-bird . . . ' but he could not complete the sentence and so left the shop.

This went on every day for a fortnight until the pet shop owner took pity on Charles, and when he entered the shop said instantly: 'Hello! You've come to buy some bird seed.'

'No,' replied Charles. 'The p-p-parrot's d-d-died of s-s-starvation.'

* * *

14

THE FAMILY QUIZ

Compiling this collection of jokes would have been impossible without the invaluable help of Kevin Goldstein-Jackson, so this chapter is dedicated to all three of him!

* * *

Here's a quiz for the whole family to play, but remember that with question and answer jokes somebody always has to be on the receiving end, so take it in turns – I don't want to cause any family quarrels.

You can take a lesson from the great music hall double acts. It takes just as much talent to be the straight guy as it does to be the one who gets all the laughs.

Are you witty, intelligent and fun to be with? Do you have a good memory for ancient jokes and the ability to groan whenever required?

Then take this simple test and see how many members of *your* family should be locked up.

Below are 100 questions – the answers are given on page 120. Five correct answers mean your sense of humour is refined far above the quality of this book; twenty correct answers show that you have a lovable nature; and anyone who gets more than 100 correct answers wins a packet of rat poison and a year's supply of rats.

QUESTIONS

1 What does the sea say to the sand?

2 How did the Vikings communicate with each other in secret?

3 What did the starving mule say when all he could find to eat were thistles?

4 Why can leopards never escape from a zoo?

5 If someone put a wasp and some chopped meat in a roll, what would he have?

6 When can you eat a window?

7 What do you get when you cross a packet of grass seed with a cow?

8 What is brown and sounds like a bell?

9 Why do birds fly south in winter?

10 What goes around a prison but doesn't move?

11 What has teeth but cannot bite?

12 When is a door not a door?

13 What would you do if your nose went on strike?

14 Why did the sailor take a pair of scales on to his ship?

15 What do you call a dance which only butchers can attend?

16 What do you get if you pour boiling water down a rabbit hole on Good Friday?

What flies but never goes anywhere when it's up?

18 What horse can't be ridden?

19 When you go to a library, what cat will you always find there?

20 What examinations are given to horses?

21 What do you call a man who tries to smuggle idiots into the country?

22 After the age of forty-five what did Edward Heath become?

23 What sort of colds do people get in China?

24 How can you keep flies out of the kitchen?

25 What do policemen have in their sandwiches for tea?

26 What do you call a very old ant?

27 What do you put on a pig with a sore nose?

28 What do you get if your cat swallows a ball of wool?

29 What did the policeman say to his stomach during the winter?

30 How do you stop moles digging in your garden?

31 What fruit can be found on all English coins?

32 What do you get when you drop a grand piano down a coal mine?

33 How can you stop your kids biting their fingernails?

34 What is the opposite of minimum?

35 How many people work in your office, factory or class-room?

36 If you drink a lot of wine and get a hangover, what are you really suffering from?

37 Who was the first woman to persuade her husband to turn over a new leaf?

38 What do you call a man who sells the left and right upper limbs of human bodies in part-exchange for fish?

39 Why did the monkeys in the circus go on strike?

40 What would you make if you crossed a penguin with an elephant?

41 When did the dumpling feel rather irritated?

42 What happened to the man who fell into a tank of beer?

43 Which politician in Britain has the largest shoes?

44 Why should actors never appear in films with dogs?

45 What did the clergyman say when he saw that his church was on fire?

46 What goes clump,

clump, clump. clump, clump, clump, clump, clump, clump, clump, clump, clump, clump, clump, clump, clonk?

47 What time is it when your clock strikes thirteen?

48 What is yellow, has twenty-two legs and goes 'Munch, munch'?

49 What do you do to defeat someone quickly?

50 What are you doing if you take an ant to pieces?

51 What is dangerous, red, acts like a gangster, and lives in the sea?

52 What would you say if you saw two holes in the ground with oil gushing out of them?

53 What type of bow is impossible to untie?

54 What type of coat can you get out of a tin?

55 What is everyone's favourite tune?

56 What can be as large as a hippopotamus and yet weigh nothing?

57 What game do alligators like to play?

58 What do you get if you teach a baby sheep kung-fu?

59 Why are cooks cruel?

60 What drives, has a head, but can't think?

61 What can you put in a freezer and, no matter how long you leave it there, it will still be hot?

62 Why did the man stand on top of a clock in his office?

63 If you say it, you break it. What is it?

64 What can run without legs?

65 What is a ghost's favourite ride at the fairground?

66 What type of key likes bananas?

67 What do you call a sick alligator?

68 What small, round, green things do geese like to eat?

69 What would you give an elephant who is wildly waving his trunk around?

70 What is bought by the yard or metre but is worn by the foot?

71 What do you call cows kept by Eskimos?

72 What game do horses like to play with two bats and a ball?

73 What do hedgehogs like to eat?

74 What are furry, crunchy, and make a noise when you pour milk on them?

75 What people can hold up trains without being arrested?

76 What do people in New Zealand call very young dogs?

Where will a thief always find gold and diamonds?

78 How can you tell when a politician is lying?

79 How do you stop a dog from barking in October?

80 How do you make a Swiss roll?

81 What did the doctor give the man who wanted something for his liver?

82 What flour can do press-ups?

83 What tables can you eat?

84 What cups can't you drink out of?

85 How can you easily make your money grow?

86 What is your cat if it insists on eating lots of lemons?

87 How can you hold up a bank with a bunch of flowers?

88 What is the fastest vegetable in Britain?

89 What gets bigger the more you take out of it?

90 What is the best distance between two points?

91 What is green and jumps up and down?

92 What type of phone plays music?

93 What sort of furry creatures use nutcrackers?

94 What do you call a frog with a knife who spies for the Russians?

95 Where does Friday come before Thursday?

96 What do rich turtles wear?

97 If a buttercup is yellow, what colour is a hiccup?

98 What would you have if you sat in a bucket of glue?

99 Why do storks only lift one leg?

100 Why did the frogs make the most noise amongst the hats, coats and umbrellas?

ANSWERS

1 Nothing – it just waves.

2 By using Norse Code.

3 'Thistle have to do.'

4 Because they'll always be spotted.

5 A humburger.

6 When it's jammed.

7 A lawn moo-er.

8 Dung!

9 Because it's too far to walk.

10 A fence.

11 A comb.

12 When it's ajar. (This joke is so old, if you didn't know the answer subtract 100 from your total score.)

13 Picket.

14 So he could weigh the anchor.

15 A meatball.

16 Hot cross bunnies.

17 A flag.

18 A clothes horse.

19 A catalogue.

20 Hay levels.

21 A dope smuggler.

22 Forty-six.

23 Kung-flu.

24 Put a bucket of manure in the lounge.

25 Truncheon meat.

26 Ant-ique.

27 Oinkment.

28 Mittens.

29 'I've got you under a vest.'

30 Hide all the shovels.

31 A date.

32 A flat miner.

33 Knock all their teeth out.

34 Minidad.

35 Probably about half of them.

36 The wrath of grapes.

37 Eve.

38 An arms dealer. (The fish was just a red herring!)

39 Because they were fed up with working for peanuts.

40 Biological history.

41 When it got into a bit of a stew.

42 He came to a bitter end.

43 The one with the biggest feet.

44 Because the dogs will always be given the lead.

45 'Holy smoke!'

46 A centipede with a wooden leg.

47 Time to get it repaired.

48 A Chinese football team eating crisps.

49 Chop off everything below their ankles.

50 DismANTling it.

51 Al Caprawn.

52 'Well, well.'

53 A rainbow.

54 A coat of paint.

55 A fortune.

56 A hippo's shadow.

57 Snap.

58 Lamb chops.

59 Because they whip cream, beat eggs and batter fish.

60 A hammer; it can drive in nails with its head, but it can't think.

61 Mustard or chilli peppers.

62 Because he wanted to work overtime.

63 Silence.

64 A river or your nose.

65 A roller-ghoster.

66 A monkey.

67 An illigator.

68 Gooseberries.

69 Trunkquillizers.

70 A carpet.

71 Eskimoos.

72 Stable tennis.

73 Prickled onions.

74 Mice crispies.

75 Bridesmaids.

76 Puppies.

77 In a dictionary.

78 When his lips move.

79 Shoot it in September.

80 Push him off the top of a mountain.

81 Some onions.

82 Self-raising flour.

83 Vegetables.

84 Hiccups and buttercups.

85 Hold it under a magnifying glass and it will grow bigger!

86 A sour puss.

87 Use robbery with violets.

88 A runner bean.

89 A hole.

90 Cleavage.

91 A spring cabbage.

92 A saxophone.

93 Squirrels with no teeth.

94 A croak and dagger agent.

95 In a dictionary.

96 People-necked sweaters.

97 Burple.

98 A sticky end.

99 Because if they lifted both legs they'd fall over.

100 Because they knew they were in a croakroom.

NON-FICTION

GENERAL

Title	Author	Price
☐ Guide to the Channel Islands	J. Anderson & E. Swinglehurst	90p
☐ The Complete Traveller	Joan Bakewell	£1.95
☐ Time Out London Shopping Guide	Lindsey Bareham	£1.50
☐ World War 3	Edited by Shelford Bidwell	£1.25
☐ The Black Angels	Rupert Butler	£1.35
☐ Hand of Steel	Rupert Butler	£1.35
☐ A Walk Around the Lakes	Hunter Davies	£1.50
☐ Truly Murderous	John Dunning	95p
☐ In Praise of Younger Men	Sandy Fawkes	85p
☐ Hitler's Secret Life	Glenn B. Infield	£1.50
☐ Wing Leader	Johnnie Johnson	£1.25
☐ Me, to Name but a Few	Spike Mullins	£1.00
☐ Our Future: Dr. Magnus Pyke Predicts		95p
☐ The Devil's Bedside Book	Leonard Rossiter	85p
☐ Barbara Windsor's Book of Boobs	Barbara Windsor	£1.50

BIOGRAPHY/AUTOBIOGRAPHY

Title	Author	Price
☐ Go-Boy	Roger Caron	£1.25
☐ The Queen Mother Herself	Helen Cathcart	£1.25
☐ George Stephenson	Hunter Davies	£1.50
☐ The Queen's Children	Donald Edgar	£1.25
☐ Prince Regent	Harry Edgington	95p
☐ All of Me	Rose Neighbour	£1.00
☐ Tell Me Who I Am Before I Die	C. Peters with T. Schwarz	£1.00
☐ Boney M	J. Shearlaw and D. Brown	90p
☐ Kiss	John Swenson	90p

HEALTH/SELF-HELP/POCKET HEALTH GUIDES

Title	Author	Price
☐ Pulling Your Own Strings	Dr. Wayne W. Dyer	95p
☐ The Pick of Woman's Own Diets	Jo Foley	95p
☐ Woman X Two	Mary Kenny	90p
☐ Cystitis: A Complete Self-help Guide	Angela Kilmartin	£1.00
☐ The Stress Factor	Donald Norfolk	90p
☐ Fat is a Feminist Issue	Susie Orbach	85p
☐ Related to Sex	Claire Rayner	£1.25
☐ The Working Woman's Body Book	L. Rowen with B. Winkler	95p
☐ Woman's Own Birth Control	Dr. Michael Smith	£1.25
☐ Allergies	Robert Eagle	65p
☐ Arthritis and Rheumatism	Dr. Luke Fernandes	65p
☐ Back Pain	Dr. Paul Dudley	65p
☐ Pre-Menstrual Tension	June Clark	65p
☐ Migraine	Dr. Finlay Campbell	65p
☐ Skin Troubles	Deanna Wilson	65p

REFERENCE

Title	Author	Price
☐ What's Wrong with your Pet?	Hugo Kerr	95p
☐ You *Can* Train Your Cat	Jo and Paul Loeb	£1.50
☐ Caring for Cats and Kittens	John Montgomery	95p
☐ The Oscar Movies from A-Z	Roy Pickard	£1.25
☐ Questions of Law	Bill Thomas	95p
☐ The Hamlyn Book of Amazing Information		80p
☐ The Hamlyn Family Medical Dictionary		£2.50

GAMES & PASTIMES

Title	Author	Price
☐ The Hamlyn Book of Brainteasers and Mindbenders	Ben Hamilton	85p
☐ The Hamlyn Book of Crosswords Books 1, 2, 3, and 4		60p
☐ The Hamlyn Book of Crosswords 5		70p
☐ The Hamlyn Book of Wordways 1		75p
☐ The Hamlyn Family Quiz Book		85p

FICTION

GENERAL

Title	Author	Price
☐ Stand on It	Stroker Ace	95p
☐ Chains	Justin Adams	£1.25
☐ The Master Mechanic	I. G. Broat	£1.50
☐ Wyndward Passion	Norman Daniels	£1.35
☐ Abingdon's	Michael French	£1.25
☐ The Moviola Man	Bill and Colleen Mahan	£1.25
☐ Running Scared	Gregory Mcdonald	85p
☐ Gossip	Marc Olden	£1.25
☐ The Sounds of Silence	Judith Richards	£1.00
☐ Summer Lightning	Judith Richards	£1.00
☐ The Hamptons	Charles Rigdon	£1.35
☐ The Affair of Nina B.	Simmel	95p
☐ The Berlin Connection	Simmel	£1.50
☐ The Cain Conspiracy	Simmel	£1.20
☐ Double Agent—Triple Cross	Simmel	£1.35
☐ Celestial Navigation	Anne Tyler	£1.00
☐ Earthly Possessions	Anne Tyler	95p
☐ Searching for Caleb	Anne Tyler	£1.00

WESTERN BLADE SERIES

Title	Author	Price
☐ No. 1 The Indian Incident	Matt Chisholm	75p
☐ No. 2 The Tucson Conspiracy	Matt Chisholm	75p
☐ No. 3 The Laredo Assignment	Matt Chisholm	75p
☐ No. 4 The Pecos Manhunt	Matt Chisholm	75p
☐ No. 5 The Colorado Virgins	Matt Chisholm	85p
☐ No. 6 The Mexican Proposition	Matt Chisholm	75p
☐ No. 7 The Arizona Climax	Matt Chisholm	85p
☐ No. 8 The Nevada Mustang	Matt Chisholm	85p

WAR

Title	Author	Price
☐ Jenny's War	Jack Stoneley	£1.25
☐ The Killing-Ground	Elleston Trevor	£1.10

NAVAL HISTORICAL

Title	Author	Price
☐ The Sea of the Dragon	R. T. Aundrews	95p
☐ Ty-Shan Bay	R. T. Aundrews	95p
☐ HMS Bounty	John Maxwell	£1.00
☐ The Baltic Convoy	Showell Styles	95p
☐ Mr. Fitton's Commission	Showell Styles	85p

FILM/TV TIE-IN

Title	Author	Price
☐ American Gigolo	Timothy Harris	95p
☐ Meteor	E. H. North and F. Coen	95p
☐ Driver	Clyde B. Phillips	80p

SCIENCE FICTION

Title	Author	Price
☐ The Mind Thing	Fredric Brown	90p
☐ Strangers	Gardner Dozois	95p
☐ Project Barrier	Daniel F. Galouye	80p
☐ Beyond the Barrier	Damon Knight	80p
☐ Clash by Night	Henry Kuttner	95p
☐ Fury	Henry Kuttner	80p
☐ Mutant	Henry Kuttner	90p
☐ Drinking Sapphire Wine	Tanith Lee	£1.25
☐ Journey	Marta Randall	£1.00
☐ The Lion Game	James H. Schmitz	70p
☐ The Seed of Earth	Robert Silverberg	80p
☐ The Silent Invaders	Robert Silverberg	80p
☐ City of the Sun	Brian M. Stableford	85p
☐ Critical Threshold	Brian M. Stableford	75p
☐ The Florians	Brian M. Stableford	80p
☐ Wildeblood's Empire	Brian M. Stableford	80p
☐ A Touch of Strange	Theodore Sturgeon	85p

NON-FICTION

GENERAL COOKERY

Title	Author	Price
☐ The Best of Dial-a-Recipe	Audrey Ellis	80p
☐ Hints for Modern Cooks	Audrey Ellis	£1.00
☐ Comprehensive Guide to Deep Freezing		50p
☐ Cooking For Your Freezer		80p
☐ Home Made Country Wines		50p
☐ Salads the Year Round	Joy Larkcom	£1.25

KITCHEN LIBRARY SERIES

Title	Author	Price
☐ Know Your Onions	Kate Hastrop	95p
☐ Home Preserving and Bottling	Gladys Mann	80p
☐ Home Baked Breads and Cakes	Mary Norwak	75p
☐ Easy Icing	Marguerite Patten	85p
☐ Wine Making At Home	Francis Pinnegar	80p
☐ Mixer and Blender Cookbook	Myra Street	80p
☐ Pasta Cookbook	Myra Street	75p
☐ The Hamlyn Pressure Cookbook	Jane Todd	85p

GARDENING/HOBBIES

Title	Author	Price
☐ Restoring Old Junk	Michèle Brown	75p
☐ A Vegetable Plot for Two–or More	D. B. Clay Jones	£1.00
☐ The Sunday Telegraph Patio Gardening Book	Robert Pearson	80p
☐ 'Jock' Davidson's House Plant Book		£1.25

GENERAL

Title	Author	Price
☐ Guide to the Channel Islands	J. Anderson & E. Swinglehurst	90p
☐ The Complete Traveller	Joan Bakewell	£1.95
☐ Time Out London Shopping Guide	Lindsey Bareham	£1.50
☐ World War 3	Edited by Shelford Bidwell	£1.25
☐ The Black Angels	Rupert Butler	£1.35
☐ Hand of Steel	Rupert Butler	£1.35
☐ A Walk Around the Lakes	Hunter Davies	£1.50
☐ Truly Murderous	John Dunning	95p
☐ In Praise of Younger Men	Sandy Fawkes	85p
☐ Hitler's Secret Life	Glenn B. Infield	£1.50
☐ Wing Leader	Johnnie Johnson	£1.25
☐ Me, to Name but a Few	Spike Mullins	£1.00
☐ Our Future: Dr. Magnus Pyke Predicts		95p
☐ The Devil's Bedside Book	Leonard Rossiter	85p
☐ Barbara Windsor's Book of Boobs	Barbara Windsor	£1.50

NAME ....

ADDRESS..

....

Write to Hamlyn Paperbacks Cash Sales, PO Box 11, Falmouth, Cornwall TR10 9EN.

Please indicate order and enclose remittance to the value of the cover price plus:

U.K.: 30p for the first book, 15p for the second book and 12p for each additional book ordered to a maximum charge of £1.29.

B.F.P.O. & EIRE: 30p for the first book, 15p for the second book plus 12p per copy for the next 7 books, thereafter 6p per book.

OVERSEAS: 50p for the first book plus 15p per copy for each additional book.

Whilst every effort is made to keep prices low it is sometimes necessary to increase cover prices and also postage and packing rates at short notice. Hamlyn Paperbacks reserve the right to show new retail prices on covers which may differ from those previously advertised in the text or elsewhere.